Jo Ryan is a registered nurse with nearly twenty years' experience, with most of her career spent working in paediatrics. She has also worked as a full-time nanny in Australia and overseas. Jo completed a Masters of Public Health, studying the health and wellbeing of women and their children in a public health context, focusing on the levels of support available to mothers of young infants within the community. As well as running her parenting support and advice service, Babybliss, she regularly appears as a parenting expert on television. Jo lives in Sydney.

# Baby bliss

## Jo Ryan

The Australian must-have guide to
sleeping, settling and establishing
routines for your baby

HarperCollins*Publishers*

# HarperCollins*Publishers*

First published in Australia in 2009
by HarperCollins*Publishers* Australia Pty Limited
ABN 36 009 913 517
www.harpercollins.com.au

Copyright © Jo Ryan 2009

The right of Jo Ryan to be identified as the author of this
work has been asserted by her under the *Copyright Amendment
(Moral Rights) Act 2000.*

**HarperCollins*Publishers***
25 Ryde Road, Pymble, Sydney, NSW 2073, Australia
31 View Road, Glenfield, Auckland 0627, New Zealand
1–A, Hamilton House, Connaught Place, New Delhi – 110 001, India
77–85 Fulham Palace Road, London, W6 8JB, United Kingdom
2 Bloor Street East, 20th floor, Toronto, Ontario M4W 1A8, Canada
10 East 53rd Street, New York NY 10022, USA

National Library of Australia Cataloguing-in-Publication data:

Ryan, Jo, 1967–
Babybliss: the Australian must-have guide to sleeping,
settling and establishing routines for your baby
ISBN: 978 0 7322 8698 9 (pbk.)
Infants — Care.
Infants — Health and hygiene.
649.122

Cover design by Darren Holt, HarperCollins Design Studio
Cover image by Max Oppenheim/Getty Images
Author photograph by Hugh Stewart
Internal design and illustrations by Alicia Freile, HarperCollins Design Studio
Typeset in 10.5 on 19pt Galliard by Kirby Jones

Printed and bound in Australia by Griffin Press

70gsm Classic used by HarperCollins*Publishers* is a natural, recyclable product made
from wood grown in sustainable forests. The manufacturing processes conform to
the environmental regulations in the country of origin, Finland

5  4  3  2  1    09  10  11  12

*For all the mothers in my life, especially my own,
and my sisters, who have always given me the best
advice, not only to do with babies.*

## Disclaimer

While this book is intended as a general information resource and all care has been taken in compiling the contents, this book does not take account of individual circumstances and this book is not in any way a substitute for professional advice. It is imperative that you always seek appropriate professional advice about parenting and health issues. The author and publisher cannot be held responsible for any claim or action that may arise from reliance on the information contained in this book.

## Note

In the interests of fairness, throughout *Babybliss*, I've alternated the use of 'he' and 'she' from section to section to refer to your baby.

# Contents

## Chapter 3

## Confident parenting 63

## Chapter 4

## Your newborn baby: the first six weeks 71

## Chapter 11

## Where to from here? 257

# Baby bliss

# INTRODUCTION

I have always been around babies and small children. I come from a large family and, as one of the eldest children, I spent a lot of time with the younger babies. I loved it and found I had a knack for reading what was going on with them — and they responded well to me. My desire to be a paediatrician was quashed pretty quickly when I realised how much study was required, and so, with a little push from my mum, I decided to study nursing when I left school.

My first hospital placement as a student nurse was on a paediatric ward and I absolutely loved it. I thought the kids were all so brave and wonderful, and although their stories were often incredibly sad, I was in awe of their resilience. And again, I found that I was able to relate to them really well.

After finishing my nursing training I decided to specialise in paediatric nursing, and so I had many wonderful years working in specialist children's hospitals. During that time I travelled overseas and worked as a live-in nanny in the United Kingdom. This is when I began to understand how demanding looking after children could be. I had many jobs, some not so wonderful, but nannying gave me a great insight to the pressures of raising a family and how relentless, but also incredibly rewarding, being a parent is.

I spent a few years working in the corporate world on my return to Australia and it was in one of these jobs that the seed was planted for my business, Babybliss. One of my bosses had a small baby, and when she discovered I was a nurse, she would ask my advice on how to deal with what her young family was going through. She happened to say to me one day how great it would be if I had a business that dealt with these problems because there really wasn't a lot of support around for new parents. It was then that I knew this was something I really wanted to do.

It was a few more years before I got up the courage to take the leap to start my own business. I studied for my Masters of Public Health in the meantime, examining support services for women and babies in a public health context, and after a life-changing, inspirational trip to Mount Everest, I decided it was time to start my Babybliss business. Now, four years later, I have worked with hundreds of families all over Australia. I deal with babies who are one day old and children who are five years old, traditional families and some families not so traditional. Every day, I learn something new from the children and from the parents. That is the best part of what I do — talking to parents, getting to know them and their family, giving advice and getting advice and hopefully making family life that little bit easier for them.

Over the years of dealing with babies and primarily working to improve their sleep issues, I have developed my own philosophy on how you can get your baby to be a great sleeper, all the while enjoying the early years without having to go through too much stress as a family. Now obviously there will always be hiccups along the way and times where you feel you have no idea what is going on. The Babybliss Settling Technique and the Babybliss philosophy give you something to fall back on during these times and some guidelines to follow through your baby's young life.

I believe that if you get the early days of your baby's life sorted, then the rest will fall into place. I don't believe in being very strict and rigid with routines while your baby is a newborn. The Babybliss Technique is all about getting to know your baby in the early days and letting him set the pace in regard to feeding and sleeping. That said, you can definitely have a plan, but rather than looking at the whole day, you look at each cycle of feeding, activity and sleep. These cycles can be anywhere between two and four hours long with a newborn, but they revolve around feeding your baby when he is hungry. This pattern will set up your milk supply, and it also means your baby will settle and sleep well after each feed.

As your baby grows you can have more of a structure to your days and nights, and by three months you should have a definite routine for your baby. The best thing about the Babybliss Technique is that it offers you an effective way of teaching your baby to be a good sleeper without having to resort to such stressful techniques as controlled crying. The technique is a gentle way to get your baby to learn to self-settle as soon as he is able to, and it encourages your child to have good sleeping patterns, as well as being happy and secure in the cot or bed at night.

We all know that mothers and fathers have an innate instinct about their children. This instinct kicks in when you first get pregnant and continues on for the whole of your child's life. Tapping into and using your instinct can really help you understand your baby, connect with him and make your way, successfully, through the challenges you may face, especially when your child is young.

There is so much information out there these days on parenting, much more so than when our parents' generation had small children. My parents had Dr Spock and that was about it. Today we have the internet for instant answers to our questions; countless books giving us contradictory methods as to the best way to bring up our children; friends, relatives, members of mothers' groups, neighbours — all spouting advice. And although I think there is a place for all that advice, I also think that *you* are the best person to work out what is best for your family. The way you do this is to watch your baby closely, observe and listen to the way he behaves and reacts to things, listen to the way he cries, notice the way he feeds and sleeps. Get a sense of who your baby is, even though he is tiny.

I really encourage you, more than anything else, more than following any routine or strategy, to really look at your baby, notice who he is and how he responds to you. If you team your innate instinct about your baby with the knowledge you will gain from this book then you will achieve the best possible experience for your young family.

The birth of a new baby is truly a blessing, but it can also be an overwhelming and difficult experience ... and that's just the delivery! Bringing your first baby home and beginning the parenting journey will affect you in ways you never imagined, and it's important not to underestimate how much your world will change.

*Babybliss* is designed to make the early stages of parenting a bit easier. Each chapter explains what you should expect during the phases of your baby's early development, with advice and tips on how to give your baby the best possible care, while caring for yourself as well. I explain some of the myths surrounding early childhood, answer frequently asked questions and provide a number of parenting alternatives, so you can decide what works best for you. Some of the things I discuss may seem obvious, but every parent's knowledge and understanding of caring for a baby is different, and it can help to have straightforward guidelines to follow.

Remember, the early months of childhood can be tiring and difficult for parents, but they are also incredibly rewarding. Be confident in your abilities, trust your parenting instincts and enjoy getting to know your new baby.

# Chapter 1

# Preparing for your baby's arrival

Before the birth, the most important physical preparation you can do is to get as much rest as possible. During pregnancy your body naturally encourages you to sleep, but most pregnant women find themselves waking up frequently during the night, either to go to the toilet or because the baby is restless.

This in itself is good training for when your sleep becomes disrupted during the first few months of your baby's life. This period can be quite intense, as newborn babies generally need to feed approximately every three hours and sometimes more frequently. So if, for example, it takes 45 minutes for your baby to feed and another 45 minutes to settle the baby, that means you have only 90 minutes to sleep before starting the process again. Not much time to feel well rested.

This amount of sleep deprivation can affect your emotional and physical wellbeing, so it's important to be healthy and rested during the pregnancy. If possible, try to nap during the day and schedule other times that you can devote to relaxation. Try not to do too much in those last few weeks before the baby's arrival. A lot of women try to squeeze everything in when they go on maternity leave. If you can, it is a great idea to start your preparations for the baby as early as possible so there is not much left to the last minute. And who knows, the baby may come early and then you will feel stressed if things like the nursery or shopping for baby supplies aren't completed.

It's also important to eat well during the pregnancy, as your doctor will have told you. A healthy, nutritious and well-balanced diet will give you and your baby the best start. It's also important to get into the habit of eating three meals a day and drinking plenty of water, as you will need to continue this practice if you will be breastfeeding your new baby.

You should also do regular, gentle exercise while you're pregnant. This is a great way to increase your energy and fitness levels, which will help with the labour and delivery and the first few months with your new baby. Exercise also increases endorphins, which make you feel better naturally and can help you sleep better at night. Remember, however, it's important to consult your doctor if you are doing any sort of exercise, especially later in your pregnancy or if there are any complications.

Another important preparation that is often overlooked is to stock up your pantry and fridge. Getting out of the house can be very difficult in the first couple of weeks and really, the last thing you will want to be doing is tackling the supermarket with a new baby and not much sleep. Fill the pantry with basic supplies and put some prepared meals in the freezer for when you just cannot find the time to cook. The best gift given to new parents is a meal, so if they ask what they can do to help, tell your family and friends that a meal would be the best thing ever!

Learning about babies is also a good idea. A lot of people go into pregnancy with very little experience with babies and small children. Read some books and watch some DVDs, but be aware there is a lot of information out there. Try to stick to one or two sources so you don't get overloaded with advice. Ask your friends and family what books and DVDs they used and follow their recommendations.

However, it is difficult for a pregnant woman to take in too much information about life *after* the delivery of her baby. A lot of people tell me I should give prenatal talks to women, which I think would be a great idea. But most women are very focused on the pregnancy, labour and delivery and won't retain too much more information. Once you get home with your baby, you realise how much you don't know about this little person. If you can, go to the talks at the hospital, do the prenatal classes and take some extra ones.

## Suggestions for exercise while pregnant

✦ Walking: gentle walking can be beneficial for both you and your baby.

✦ Yoga: this is a great prenatal exercise and most yoga centres offer pregnancy classes. There are also yoga DVDs available so you can practice at home.

+ Aqua aerobics or water aerobics: most swimming centres offer regular classes.

+ Swimming: either at home or at the local pool. Swimming is a great exercise as it relieves the heaviness you might be feeling in your body.

+ Gentle aerobics: most gyms offer pregnancy classes and there are lots of DVDs available.

Remember when exercising:

+ Always check with your doctor first that it is okay to do the kind of exercise you want to do.

+ Drink plenty of water and avoid getting too hot.

+ Don't let yourself get fatigued. The exercise should be refreshing but not punishing.

+ Don't exercise every day. Three times a week is plenty — you need to have rest days.

+ Don't do any exercise that requires you to lie flat on your back after the first three months.

+ Don't set any personal bests. Your body is busy doing other things at the moment. Always stop when you feel fatigued.

## How can I mentally prepare?

The most important thing to know is that your life will not be the same once this little person arrives. A lot of parents-to-be like to think that their life will not change that much after having one baby, but this is really not the case. You need to know and accept that things will be different but different in a good way.

Before the birth most parents-to-be experience excitement, fear and anticipation. The fear and anxiety can be alleviated by being prepared. But it is also good to know that things might not go according to your plans. I tell expectant mothers that it is a great idea to have a birth plan but to be prepared to accept that the birth might not happen that way and they will need to then let go of their expectations and go with whatever happens.

Talk to your partner about how you are feeling so you are both aware of what is going on for each other. Share your feelings and your anxieties. When you bring your new baby home things will change between you and your partner as the dynamic in the house will be different. It will no longer be just you two, there will be another person to consider. And this person, although the littlest in the house, will demand the most attention. So talk about this beforehand. Discuss how things like night feeding and nappy changing will work.

Also have a plan to keep things quiet and calm during the first four to six weeks. You will need to have a statement ready for when the hordes of relatives and friends want to descend on you. It is really important to stay as close to home as you can in those first few weeks and keep the visitors to a minimum. Your new baby needs to get to know you both and you need to get to know her. You need to navigate your way through the first couple of weeks and the last thing you need is dozens of visitors confusing you with their advice — as good as it might be.

# How do I get my other children ready for the new baby?

If your new baby has older siblings, it's important to tell them about the new baby before he arrives, maybe a month or two before the birth. Young children generally can't grasp the concept of time, so if you tell them too far in advance they may wear you down with daily questions about when the baby is coming or why the baby hasn't come yet. If your older child notices your stomach getting larger, however, this is a good opportunity to explain that a baby is growing inside so your child can start getting used to the baby's existence.

Older siblings, depending on their age, can react differently to the birth of a new baby. Some may be excited, some may be indifferent and others may be resentful. Around the time of the birth, it can be a good idea to give an older sibling a gift 'from' the newborn, as this often makes the child more interested in getting to know their new brother or sister.

You can also prepare your older child for the new arrival by:

✦ reading books to them about brothers and sisters
✦ including them in deciding your baby's name
✦ taking them with you on doctor or midwife visits

+ visiting friends or relatives with new babies
+ encouraging friendships with other children, as it's important for children to have a close playmate
+ explaining your visit to hospital by telling them you will be away for a while but will return after the baby has arrived
+ organising for someone who your older child knows and trusts to care for them while you are in hospital, which can reduce feelings of separation anxiety while you are away.

After the baby arrives, giving your older child the attention he needs can be quite difficult. Playing together is hard when you're constantly nursing, feeding or attending to your newborn, but it's important not to use your new baby as an excuse for spending less time with your older child. Try scheduling some one-on-one time each day during some of the new baby's frequent sleeps.

You may find that your older child will regress slightly after the baby arrives and this is very normal. For example, a child that is completely toilet trained may start to wet the bed at night again. You should not get upset or angry with your child if this happens. Just deal with the behaviour as you did in the past and eventually the older child will regain the lost skill.

Behaviour in older children can also go off for a bit after the birth of a new baby. I often get calls from mothers perplexed about why their two year old, who has always been a great sleeper, all of a sudden won't go to bed and is screaming the place down. When I ask them when this behaviour began it usually coincided with the birth of the new baby. The mothers then tell me that the older child absolutely adores the baby, so why would he be acting out? Although older children might not display any animosity towards the baby, things for them have changed. Their world is now very different and they don't know why and you can't explain it to them. So they may not relate it directly to the baby but they will often display it by behaving differently from the way they did before the baby arrived.

In dealing with this behaviour change you need to take into consideration that your older child's world has changed and you are no longer completely available to him. Be gentle and understanding but maintain good boundaries and don't let the child get away with bad behaviour just because he is getting used to this new person in his life. Have a good routine and stick with it.

# How do I get my pet(s) to adjust to the new baby?

If you have pets, it's important to be careful around them while you're pregnant. Avoid touching animal faeces or cat litter boxes as these can be a source of toxoplasmosis, a disease that domestic animals carry in their excrement from eating wildlife, and which can also come from eating undercooked meat. If you need to clean up after cats or dogs, be sure to wear gloves and wash your hands thoroughly.

After your baby is born, there's no reason why she can't coexist with your pets, as long as you're careful and vigilant at all times. Like older siblings, it's important to introduce the pet and the baby so the pet can become used to having a new person in the house. Be sure to keep pets out of the baby's room, especially cats who like sleeping in warm places like prams or cots. Your pet may display signs of 'sibling rivalry' when the new baby arrives and your attention is no longer completely devoted to them. As with older children, try to spend some one-on-one time with your pet every day and avoid disrupting their usual routine, which includes walks and playtime.

## Essential baby equipment

Before the birth it is important to prepare your home with everything your baby will need, as the last thing you'll want to do while dealing with a newborn is shop for a pram. A lot of baby essentials will only be used for a short time, so try to borrow as much as you can from friends and family. If you're planning to have a baby shower, your guests will undoubtedly give you various baby essentials, so try to avoid doubling up. Things like breast pumps can also be hired from chemists and baby-hire companies, which can ease the financial burden and also reduce the clutter in your home when you no longer need them.

Before investing in expensive items like prams and cots, it is a good idea to do some research into the different options and ask other parents what worked best for them. When it comes to buying these items, many people fall into the trap of choosing the latest or most fashionable models, but they are not always the most suitable or user friendly.

Your new baby is going to need loads of nappies, baby wraps and very important items like burping cloths. Stock up with more than you expect to need, rather than running out in those first few weeks. Disposable nappies are far easier and more convenient to use than cloth nappies, but are not as environmentally friendly. Work out which option is best for you.

The following pages provide a checklist of all the things you will probably need for your baby's first few months.

## The nursery

✦ Cot or bassinette with a firm, well-fitted mattress. Only purchase cots that meet Australian standards. All cots that meet the standard will be clearly labelled AS 2172. If you borrow a cot it is important that it also meets Australian standards. Lead paint, gaps that a baby can get caught in and sides that are too low are risks associated with using second-hand cots.

✦ Wardrobe and/or chest of drawers for the baby's clothes.

✦ Comfortable chair with a straight back for you to sit in while feeding, but it might be worthwhile to wait until you get home to test out what works best for you and your baby.

✦ Baby monitor. There is actually no evidence that baby-breathing monitors, or apnoea monitors, protect your baby from SIDS. In fact breathing monitors can make parents' life more stressful as there are often false alarms. If your doctor has suggested a breathing monitor then of course use one, but I would recommend that you use a sound monitor. Again, these can cause stress as they amplify every little noise your baby makes. So if your baby is sleeping not that far from where you are then I would suggest turning it off or at least having the sound turned down low if you feel more comfortable having one.

✦ Heater or fan, depending on the season. These must be placed well away from the baby's bed.

✦ Music. There are loads of CDs available with settling sounds and music for babies. However, a radio will do just as well.

✦ Night-light. Babies can sleep in pitch dark but a night-light will help you see what you are doing during night feeding. A dimmer on the main light switch is just as good, or a lamp in the corner of the room.

## Clothing

✦ Six cotton singlets or all-in-one bodysuits. It's best to buy a few in size 0000 and a few in size 000, but if your doctor has confirmed your baby will be large at birth, you probably won't need any in 0000 size. As your baby grows, you will need a few more singlets or all-in-one suits in 000 size. If you are having your baby in winter there are also merino wool singlets and suits available.

✦ Four to six stretch towelling all-in-one babysuits, some in size 0000 and some in size 000. Buying a few short-sleeved suits is a good idea if the weather will be warm during your baby's first few months. Suits that have the feet in them help with babies' comfort and sleeping in the early days.

✦ Four to six pairs of socks or bootees. Bootees are not around much these days as they are handknitted.

✦ One pair of scratch mittens. These are little cotton mittens to put on when babies are tiny so they don't scratch themselves with their sharp little fingernails.

✦ One or two cardigans or hooded jackets for colder months.

✦ Three newborn-size bibs.

✦ One summer hat.

✦ Other clothes for going out.

## Feeding

✦ Two or three maternity feeding bras.

✦ Disposable breast pads. One box to start with and then see what you need.

✦ Six to eight washable breast pads (optional). Re-usable breast pads can be washed over and over again, and so are more cost-effective.

✦ Breast pump for expressing milk. Avent and Medela both make excellent manual pumps, or you can hire electric ones from chemists or through baby-hire companies.

- Bottles or bags for storing breast milk. Avent and Medela both offer good plastic-bag systems for storing breast milk; zip-lock bags can also be used and are much more cost-effective.
- Steriliser. Microwavable sterilisers are quick and convenient but not as large as others that plug into a power source.
- Breastfeeding pillow. There are quite a few of these on the market, although often a pillow or a cushion you already have can be a better option.
- Bottles and teats for bottle-fed babies.
- Twelve cloth nappies to use as burping cloths and cleaning cloths.

## Sleeptime

- Three sets of 100 per cent cotton sheets, sized to fit the cot or bassinette.
- One or two 100 per cent cotton blankets, sized to fit the cot or bassinette.
- One woollen blanket for colder months, sized to fit the cot or bassinette.
- One or two waterproof mattress protectors.
- Cotton wraps, either muslin or stretch cotton. I actually prefer the stretch cotton wraps in a large size (120 x 120 cm) as they are easier to wrap up a baby nice and firmly.
- Dummy, to have on hand just in case.

## Bathtime

- Baby bath. If you don't have enough space for a baby bath, you can bathe your baby in a sink, tub or regular bath (this is discussed further in Chapter 2).
- Three baby towels. These often have a hood to dry the baby's head.
- Three or four soft cotton washcloths. Muslin squares can also be used.
- Baby wash and baby oil or cream. I am of the belief that less is best, so don't buy too many of these products, and try to use products with little or no fragrance.
- Baby nail clippers or scissors. Scissors are a better option than clippers as they are less clumsy to use.
- Bath toys. As your baby gets bigger it is nice for him to have something to look at while he is in the bath and eventually he will start to grab for the toys.
- Bath thermometer.
- Cotton buds.
- Baby massage oil.

## Playtime

- Playmat or baby gym. These are not important until about eight weeks of age so hold off on buying them till a bit later if you want.
- Rocker or bouncer. Try to borrow these as they are an item that you won't use for too long.

+ Mobile for hanging over the change table or rocker/bouncer.
+ Other toys suitable for babies aged from newborn to six months, such as rattles, soft animals and dolls, music boxes and teethers.

## Nappies

+ Thirty-six newborn disposable nappies or 24 cloth nappies. Your baby will usually need a nappy change every time you feed him, so expect to use six to 12 in 24 hours. You might go through two per feed as it is a baby's prerogative to dirty his nappy as soon as he has a clean one on.
+ Cleaning basics such as disposable wipes, cotton balls, zinc-based barrier cream and anti-rash powder. I am a huge believer in the less-is-best theory when it comes to babies, and as they come to you in perfect condition there is no need to put creams and the like on their skin unless there is a problem.
+ Wipe-clean change mat or washable change pad.
+ Baby change table. You may prefer to use a padded change mat on an existing table.
+ Storage for nappies, creams and other items. This can be a basket or a set of drawers near the change table.
+ Nappy bags or a bin for disposable nappies. The nappy bin is a fabulous invention that eliminates the need to fill the kitchen bin with dirty nappies. There are quite a few nappy bins on the market but they do take up floor space. If you are short of space then the scented bags might be the better way to go. These can be purchased from the supermarket.

## Out and about

✦ Pram, with a rain/sun cover. There is an enormous number of prams on the market these days. Ask your friends what prams they have and would they recommend them. Things to consider when choosing a pram include:
  – what sort of car you have and how big the boot is
  – where you will be taking your baby and will the pram be manoeuvrable in and out of shops/cafés etc.
  – find out what accessories you need with the pram (ask around what accessories are best to have) and if they come as standard or will cost you extra
  – if you travel a lot then take that into consideration as a lot of prams are too big to take on planes
  – if you exercise and want to run with your baby in the pram.

✦ Sling or carrier. BabyBjörn offers an excellent baby carrier. There are many slings on the market so test them out before you buy.

✦ Car baby capsule. These are suitable for use until approximately six months of age, or a convertible car seat that can be used for newborns to four year olds. I recommend hiring the baby capsule as you only really need one temporarily. Baby capsules can be hired from many different places and these vary from state to state. In some states, maternity hospitals will hire and fit them. If you are unsure, it would be a good idea to ask your maternity hospital where is the best place to hire, or check with Kidsafe.

✦ Child restraint. You will eventually have to purchase a child restraint for the car. These can be used from birth if they are the convertible type or once your baby has reached eight kilograms. Any child restraint you purchase should carry the Australian standard AS 1754 label. You also need to make sure the restraint you purchase is suitable for your car, especially if it is a small car or an older vehicle. If you are unsure, seek advice from your local transport authority or motoring organisation, or check with Kidsafe.

✦ Head support for the baby capsule.

✦ Car window shade.

✦ Transport bag for your pram, if the pram needs to go on a plane as luggage.

✦ Nappy bag. This is a bag to put all the baby's things in when you leave the house and can be any medium to large bag that's easy to carry, preferably one with long handles that can go over your shoulder.

## Basic first aid

✦ Baby paracetamol or some other medicine used to reduce temperatures and pain. Ask your doctor or paediatrician what they recommend.

✦ Thermometer.

## Preparing for twins or multiple births

Preparation for twins or multiples is almost the same as for a single baby, but they are more likely to be born earlier and they may be smaller than a single baby. You are also more likely to have a caesarean birth, depending on the position of the babies in the womb. It's a good idea to get plenty of rest, read all you can about multiple births and organise some help at home, as it will be very hard to be on your own in the first few months with two or more tiny babies. Having more than one baby is also very tiring as your down-time can be short. Mothers of twins and multiples get less sleep than mothers of single babies, which can make life more stressful along with the extra expense that having two or more babies carries.

It is really important to not try to be superwoman! If someone offers you help then take it. Meals, cleaning, assisting with settling, bathing or changing the babies, even just making a cup of tea for you is a relief to a sleep-deprived mother of two or more tiny babies.

Twins and multiples often come earlier than single babies, so be prepared that little bit earlier. Make sure everything is ready for the babies at around 35 weeks. With twins you will need almost double everything you would buy for a single baby, especially regarding clothing, nappies and car seats. With cots, however, I recommend you put the babies together in one full-size cot for a couple of months. These babies have been so close for nine months that it is not a great idea to separate them when they are little, so you can hold off on buying another cot or cots until further down the track.

If you are having twins, you will need to purchase a twin pram. After working with many sets of newborn twins, the recommendation I hear the most is for the side-by-side pram rather than the pram where one baby sits behind the other. You also should test-run a few prams and take the measurements because they can be really wide and might not fit in your car or through your front door.

Breastfeeding twins and multiples can be challenging so it is a good idea to get in touch with the Australian Breastfeeding Association (ABA) (www.breastfeeding.asn.au), a private lactation consultant or the Australian Multiple Birth Association (AMBA) (www.amba.org.au) before the babies arrive to discuss your options and have some support ready.

## Organising the household for the first few weeks

The first few weeks of a baby's life can be the most overwhelming for parents, especially for those who are new to parenthood, so it's often a good idea to accept any help that is offered. Both parents should spend as much time as possible at home with the baby during the first month so they can bond with their new child, as well as become accustomed to the different schedules and tasks involved in parenthood.

If your partner is unable to be at home during that period, another family member or friend may offer to stay with you or visit often to help out with the baby. If this is the case, your focus should be on caring for the baby, while the other person assists with such things as housework, cooking, grocery shopping and making you that much-needed cup of tea. If having another person in the house is causing you undue stress, however, it's best to thank them for their help but explain that you'd prefer to manage alone.

As I mentioned earlier, have plenty of prepared meals stacked in the freezer as these are the best way to get the food you need with little stress, and anyone can prepare them. It is important that you eat well, so keep that freezer well stocked and accept any offers of having a meal cooked for you. It is also a good idea to get a cleaner to come in, even just once a fortnight to assist with the heavier cleaning of the house. Or if this is not possible ask a friend to come and help you, even to just hold the baby, while you get things in order. But I do tell mothers that something usually has to give in the early days, and the best thing to let go of is the housework. Try not to stress too much if things are not looking so neat around the place. The mess will still be there tomorrow and you can fix it later. The most important thing is that you and the baby are getting plenty of food and plenty of sleep.

If you are the parent of newborn twins or multiples, accept any help that is offered. It is extremely difficult to look after two or more newborn babies on your own so if your partner cannot be home with you for the first month, ask a relative to come and stay or visit daily. There are mothercraft nurses or nannies you can hire, or AMBA can assist you in finding support in your area.

## 'You' time

Although this period can be extremely busy and overwhelming, it is really important to make sure you have some time for yourself. Whether this be when the baby is sleeping or in the evening when your partner is home, it is a great idea to do this thing every day so it becomes your little ritual. For some mothers it may be as simple as having a long shower or bath, reading the paper, or watching a bit of *Oprah* in the afternoon. 'You' time can also include the baby if you can't manage anything else. A walk around the block or to the shops to get that morning coffee is just as good.

In the early days it can be difficult to plan your days as most babies are on a three- to four-hourly feeding schedule but this can be a two-hour schedule on some days. In these early days it is better to let the baby set the routine, that way you will be more relaxed about feeding and sleeping times. Trying to follow a really strict schedule with a newborn baby can lead to lots of unnecessary problems with feeding and sleeping.

I teach mothers to have a flexible routine around feeding and then the baby should sleep until she is next due to feed, which can be between two and four hours after the beginning of the last feed. Just knowing this can give you some idea of how your day and night will be. Trying to follow a really strict routine that dictates specific times of the day for feeding and sleeping will set you up to fail as it imposes unreasonable expectations on your baby and her ability to stay awake and stay asleep.

Remember to make a little time for yourself every day — that way you will retain a sense of normality when you might feel that everything else is really different and unpredictable.

# SIDS information

◆ Sudden Infant Death Syndrome is very rare. The cause is unknown.

◆ It affects about 1 in 1300 infants.

◆ It occurs more in the winter months and colder climates, in low socioeconomic families and in premature babies.

◆ SIDS is most common in babies between one and six months of age.

◆ Cigarette smoke can increase the risk of SIDS.

# Prevention of SIDS

+ Put your baby down to sleep on her back.
+ Make sure your baby's face is uncovered.
+ Use a firm, clean mattress that fits the cot well.
+ Keep quilts, doonas, duvets, pillows and cot bumpers out of the cot to reduce the risk of smothering.
+ Position the baby's feet at the bottom of the cot and tuck the bedclothes in securely.
+ Don't expose your baby to cigarette smoke before and after birth.

# Chapter 2

# The new person in your life

Leaving the hospital with your new baby can be a very daunting experience. Although being in hospital can be a bit overwhelming and confusing — you will find that most midwives have their own ideas on how to do things and no two will be the same — walking in your front door with a brand-new baby can provoke extreme feelings. I have had parents tell me that they have walked through the door and burst out laughing, completely surprised that anyone would let them leave the hospital, on their own, with a tiny little baby, without any supervision. Others have told me that they were terrified when they got home, with absolutely no idea what to expect in the next 12 hours, let alone the next 12 years! All these feelings are completely normal and very common, so don't be alarmed if you feel a bit out of your league on that first day at home.

The best way of coping with the first couple of days is to have everything you need ready at home so you don't have to go out if you don't want to. Make sure the freezer and fridge are full and keep the visitors to a minimum. This time is for you and your baby to get to know each other. It is time for her to get used to her new surroundings and you both to get used to this new person in your home.

And try to go with it a bit. Remember that it will be overwhelming and you might not know what to do but it is just like starting a new job. It will take some time to settle in and get used to your new responsibilities but you will get the hang of it soon. There's no need to put pressure on yourselves to be perfect parents from day one. If you are completely terrified about those first few days at home, ask someone you trust to come and help out. Be it a family member or a professional, their support can help you all to settle in and build your confidence in dealing with the baby.

## How to deal with the baby blues

Many mothers experience the 'baby blues' to a certain degree, and it's perfectly natural to do so. Common symptoms include frustration, anger, sadness and the feeling that you're unable to cope. The baby blues usually start at around three to five days after the birth, when the mother begins to produce milk, and can last about a week.

If these feelings last any longer, and if you continue to be highly emotional or experience a lack of interest in the baby, this can signal the early signs of postnatal depression (PND). Although PND is quite common, it's important to address it early by discussing how you feel with your partner and consulting your doctor.

One thing to remember is that early parenthood is a time of extreme change, both physically and emotionally, and you are dealing with this while being completely sleep deprived. You may find yourself crying a lot, which is a normal reaction when you're tired and stressed. It's important that you eat well and get enough rest so you can function and think properly. It's also a good idea to try to rest when your baby is asleep — for example, during the baby's morning or afternoon nap. If you're unable to nap during these short times when your baby is asleep, use your rest time to read a magazine or watch TV, or anything that gives you some time out.

If you can avoid it, it's a good idea in the early weeks not to spend all your rest time on housework, cooking or other chores. The most important thing is to spend as much time as possible bonding with your baby, resting and getting used to your new parenting routine. Asking your partner, a friend or a family member for help with the household chores and errands can help ease the burden, but if nobody is available, don't worry if you fall behind. Nobody will mind if the house is not in tip-top shape while you're caring for your newborn.

New fathers can also experience some PND, which can be more common when their partner has PND. Men often find it difficult to talk about their feelings and don't express how the changes that are happening with the arrival of a new baby are affecting them. They can feel stress about financial matters with a new person to consider, as well as most likely having to work during the day after not getting much sleep at night.

As with all first symptoms of PND, it is really important to seek professional help. Your GP or baby health clinic nurse is a great first course of action. If you are unsure about what you are feeling you should talk to your family or friends and, of course, your partner.

That said, it is completely normal to feel out of your depth in the first few weeks. New mothers can prepare for their baby like they are tackling a new project at work. Research is done, plans are written, lists are made. While this is all great and it is a good idea to read parenting books before you have your baby, don't overdo it. Don't read every book in the parenting section. Ask your friends who have had babies what books they found most beneficial and go for those ones. Also try not to have too strict an idea of how those first few weeks will be or stick to a routine that you have decided will work for you. In most cases it is usually the mothers who have a very definite idea of what their baby will be like and how it will sleep and eat and so on who really struggle in the first couple of months. Your baby is going to be unique, with his own little personality and you *can't* predict what will happen until you have spent some time getting to know him. So put the plans aside for a bit. Read the books and talk to other mothers about what the first couple of months are like. But try not to freak yourself out too much either, as a lot of people will only give you the horror stories. Those first months will be hard and you will be very tired, but it is also a fantastic, wonderful and very special time in your life. As much as you can, you need to enjoy it too.

# What will my baby do?

Many new parents are surprised at just how inactive newborns are. They're tiny, pinkish creatures that lie about with their limbs dangling, doing little more than pooing, weeing, eating and sleeping. Most newborns are curled up like little koalas at first from spending so long in such a small, cramped uterus and may take a few weeks to fully uncurl and stretch out.

As babies' reflexes start to develop, they start working their facial muscles, which means a lot of unintentional smiles, grimaces and funny faces. They are also prone to gurgling and making strange noises, so don't be surprised if your baby sometimes sounds a bit like a small animal in the middle of the night.

Babies generally wet their nappies every time they feed, so be sure to have at least 12 clean nappies ready to use for each 24-hour period. Lots of wet nappies are a good sign that your baby is getting enough milk. As for pooing, the frequency can vary depending on how your baby is feeding. In the early weeks, breastfed babies may poo once or twice every feed, whereas for bottle-fed babies it may only be once every day or two. For bottle-fed babies, as long as the baby's poo is soft, smooth and pasty, anything more frequent than once every 48 hours is usually normal. If your baby is producing small, hard, rock-like poo, however, it may mean she is constipated and it's worthwhile consulting your doctor. Also be aware that formula-fed babies can be prone to constipation.

'Colic' is a term often bandied around, usually by older generations, like the grandmothers who use it to describe any unsettled behaviour in a baby. The term is overused, and often an unsettled baby is just restless for no logical reason — which can be very frustrating. It is also equally common for babies to be unsettled regardless of whether they're breastfed or bottle-fed.

Crying is common for new babies and can usually be attributed to a few things:

+ hunger
+ tiredness
+ a dirty or wet nappy.

These are the three most common reasons for a new baby to cry, and the problem that is most overlooked is your baby's tiredness. New babies need an enormous amount of sleep, and I'll discuss this in detail on pages 72–85.

## Dealing with visitors

Once you are home from hospital, things can be quite overwhelming. You may feel like you have everything under control or you may feel a bit all over the place. I think it is important for you to get your confidence, and for you and your baby to get used to each other.

Of course, you will want to show off your new addition to your family and friends but I recommend keeping those visits to a minimum, especially in the first couple of weeks you are back at home.

Schedule people to pop in around the same time, and keep visitors to a set number every couple of days. That way you won't have people in the house all day and you can concentrate on getting the baby fed and settled without other pairs of eyes watching your every move.

Breastfeeding can be difficult at first and a lot of women like to do it on their own with little distraction. The last thing you need is a room full of people watching you try to attach this little thing who is screaming to be fed. It will only make you flustered and panicked. Also, you may not want to get your breasts out in front of your friends or family, and you don't want to have to make the baby wait too long for that feed.

So set some boundaries, get your partner to be the gate-keeper, and don't be afraid to ask people to visit you at another time. Your baby is not going anywhere; there will be plenty of time for family and friends to have a cuddle with your new addition.

## When to call a doctor

When babies get sick they do it very quickly, so it's important to know what the first signs or symptoms are. Usually when a baby is unwell, especially a very young baby, one of the first symptoms can be that she is not as interested in her feed. You might find she won't take any of the feed or only a small amount.

A sick baby can also become quite sleepy and listless. If you find it difficult to wake her or she just won't stay awake for the whole feed *or* she is very floppy, then you should seek medical advice.

A baby who cries for very long periods of time can be unwell. Babies do cry but if she is crying for most of the day or her cry is different from what it normally is, and she is not feeding well or has any other abnormality, it is advisable to take her to a doctor.

And, of course, a sick baby might have a raised temperature. Normal body temperature is about 36.5°C to 37°C. Anything under about 37.5°C is considered okay, however. There are medications on the market for babies that reduce a fever but if your baby is very young and there are no indications as to why she might have a fever, then it is advisable to seek medical attention.

If you are unsure about whether or not your baby is sick, it is worth taking her to see a GP. It is far better to be safe than sorry. Children's hospitals will always prioritise a small baby and so she will be seen very soon after you arrive. If you feel there is something wrong with your baby then you need to act upon that feeling. As the mother you will have an innate sense about your child and rather than second-guess yourself I advise getting your baby looked at rather than waiting until she is very unwell. And if there is nothing wrong with her, then that's great.

## Feeding

Breastfeeding your baby is a wonderful, bonding experience. But it is important to understand that breastfeeding is a learnt skill for you and your baby and can take some time to get to the point where you feel as though you have mastered it. Some women take to it like a duck to water and others can have a more difficult introduction and may also have some ongoing challenges. Be reassured that most breastfeeding problems can be solved and there is help available if you are struggling.

If you are finding breastfeeding a bit difficult once you are home then get some help sooner rather than later. The longer you go on with it not being right, the worse your nipples might become and your milk supply might be affected, so get onto it quickly.

Breastfeeding has many benefits for both you and your baby.

## Benefits of breastfeeding for baby

+ Breast milk provides all the nutrients a baby needs for about the first six months of life.
+ Breast milk provides resistance to disease by:
  - providing antibodies to fight infections
  - lessening the risk of your baby getting allergies and asthma

– protecting your baby from common illnesses such as colds, diarrhoea and ear infections

– helping to reduce the risk of SIDS.

Breastfed babies also have a lower risk of developing juvenile diabetes, childhood cancers and possible heart disease later in life and can have enhanced eyesight, intelligence, speech and jaw development.

## Benefits of breastfeeding for mother

✦ Breastfeeding helps the uterus return to its pre-pregnant state and can assist with weight loss.

✦ Breastfeeding usually delays the return of menstruation.

✦ Exclusive breastfeeding can act as a contraceptive (but should not be relied upon as the only form of contraceptive).

✦ Breastfeeding protects the mother's health, especially in the long term, with reduced rates of breast and ovarian cancer, and osteoporosis.

# Bathing

Because newborn babies don't really do much in the first few weeks of their life, they don't have much of a chance to get dirty. Fitting bathtime into your busy day can be difficult, so don't be alarmed if you can only bath your baby once every two to three days. Babies make most of their mess in their nappies, so cleaning your baby with a damp washcloth or nappy wipe during every nappy change will cover most of her washing needs.

After the birth, the midwife at the hospital or birthing centre will demonstrate how to bath your baby. At home you can use a plastic baby bath, a sink, a tub or a regular bathtub. Bending over a bath can be quite tiring, so it's best to use a high sink or a bath on legs that will allow you to stand up during bathtime. Laundry tubs can be good too, as these are often deep enough to allow you to hold the baby upright while bathing. Babies also love being floated in warm, deep water.

It's important that the bath water is the right temperature for your baby, which is between 36°C and 38°C. Babies tend to like it on the hotter end of that scale rather than cooler. Don't be afraid to make the bath really nice and warm as this can put your baby into a state of euphoria and assist them to sleep well afterwards. Filling the bath quite deep means you'll be able to float your baby (while supporting her underneath) and rock her back and forth in the water, which is a useful settling technique. Many babies find this action soothing enough for them to nod off, so it's a good idea to schedule bathtime just before your baby is due for a sleep, or if she is particularly unsettled.

It is really important to keep your baby safe while bathing, so a few things to remember are:

✦ Always stay with your baby while she is in the bath.

✦ Make sure the water temperature is between 36°C and 38°C before you put your baby in the bath.

✦ Get everything you'll need during and after the bath ready before you put the baby in the water, such as a washcloth, towel, clean nappy and clothes.

After bathing, massage is another great way to help settle your baby. Apply a small amount of natural oil or baby massage oil to the baby's body, arms and legs and rub it gently into the skin. Massage is a great way to help your baby relax before sleep. It can also help parents and babies to bond, as well as provide an opportunity for fathers or non-primary care-givers to spend quality time with the baby. Bathing your baby is an excellent bonding experience, so it's good for both parents to be involved as much as possible.

## Nappy changing

New babies generally wet or dirty their nappies eight to ten times in a 24-hour period. The smell will probably give it away, but otherwise you should check the nappy every couple of hours or at least every feed. Nappies generally need to be changed when babies wake and it's often a good idea to change your baby in the middle of a feed. The reason for this is because babies often fall asleep during their feeds, so a nappy change can help wake them up again. Obviously you need to stop the feed while changing your baby, and don't be alarmed if your baby wets or dirties the nappy as soon as you restart the feed — this is very normal, they seem to like to do it in a clean nappy.

Baby urine is quite acidic and can cause nappy rash, as can poo if it is left on the baby's skin for a while. If a rash has formed, lightly rub nappy rash cream, barrier cream or zinc onto the affected area. Babies' skin is otherwise clean and unblemished so if there is no rash, there's no need to apply cream during changing as over-application of these creams may cause irritation. Your baby's skin is perfect so you don't need to try to improve on that!

A lot of new parents have never changed a nappy before they are faced with changing their own baby's. It may be a good idea to practise on a friend's or relative's baby first to understand the technique. Disposable nappies come in distinct sizes and if your baby is small the nappy may be too large for it. The nappy should be put on firmly with the tabs pulled across the baby's stomach to secure it. Cloth nappies can be tricky to attach properly, so a rehearsal for both Mum and Dad is a good idea.

# Sleeping

Deciding where your baby will sleep is a matter of personal preference. The amount of space you have at home will also be a factor, so it's important to work out the best option for you and your family.

A lot of parents prefer to have their baby sleep close to the mother in the parents' room during the first six weeks or so. It has been suggested that this reduces the risk of SIDS, as the baby's breathing is regulated by the mother's breathing. This option provides a good opportunity to bond with your new baby and get used to its sounds and habits. Having your newborn baby sleep with you is also a good idea if the nursery isn't close to your bedroom. Babies can be quite noisy sleepers, however, and they make all kinds of different noises when they sleep, from grunting and snorting through to little billy-goat bleats, so after a few weeks of sharing a bedroom you may prefer to move the baby to the nursery or another room nearby.

I am not a huge fan of co-sleeping because it is not really safe, and also it is not especially restful for anyone — baby or parents. Co-sleeping is not safe as there is a risk of smothering your baby. Exhaustion and sleep deprivation can mean that you will drop into a very deep sleep when you do go to sleep and there have been incidents of parents rolling on their babies and not being aware until it was too late. I know some parents love having their babies in their bed and that decision is completely yours, obviously, but I have dealt with so many babies whose parents decide at six, ten or 12 months that they now want the baby out of their bed and that can be a difficult adjustment for the baby. They have spent a significant amount of their life being so close to Mum. It can be a massive change for them to then sleep on their own, in their own cot.

Cots and bassinettes are both suitable for newborns to sleep in. Also, many modern prams have inbuilt bassinettes where the baby can sleep until he is old enough to move into a cot. A newborn baby finds it more comfortable to sleep in a smaller bed when they first get home from hospital as they are so used to being in small space, so I do recommend putting your baby in a bassinette initially. If they go into a big cot straightaway they can get a little unsettled and might not be happy about going to bed. A big space may frighten them at first.

When buying or borrowing the cot, whether it is new or second-hand, make sure it bears a label saying it meets the Australian standard for cots (AS 2172). Babies can become trapped in a tilted rocking cradle or bassinette, so if the cradle, bassinette or cot rocks, be sure it has a locking pin and is secured in place. The cot or bassinette should have a firm, well-fitted mattress, a fitted bottom sheet, a top sheet and a single blanket in colder months. Avoid any superfluous bedding like pillows, quilts, doonas, duvets and lambskins. These are unnecessary and may cover the baby's face and prevent him from breathing easily and sleeping comfortably. You should also avoid using cot bumpers.

A lot of people also use hammocks to put their babies in. These are okay as long as they have a firm base or mattress and the baby's face is not too close to the hammock edges. You need to make sure that the baby is secure and won't roll or slip while in the hammock.

Your baby should be swaddled or wrapped cosily in a baby wrap and tucked under the top sheet and blanket with his face uncovered. The amount of swaddling and the weight of the material used to wrap the baby will depend on the season and the temperature of the room.

The cot or bassinette should be free of toys and other items like hanging mobiles that attract the baby's attention. Rather than soothing the baby, these items can overstimulate the senses and make it difficult for the baby to get to sleep, so it's best to keep the sleeping area as plain as possible. If you have a mobile, hanging it over the change table will keep your baby occupied while you change nappies.

There are a few things to keep in mind when deciding on where your baby will sleep:

✦ Your baby could be very noisy when she sleeps, so if one of you, or both of you are particularly averse to noise or are light sleepers you may want the baby to sleep in her own room.

✦ You will be up during the night every two to three hours so it's good if the baby is somewhere close to you, especially if it is in the colder months of the year.

## Sleeping position and bedding

There are a couple of really important things parents need to know about safe sleeping for their new baby. These are:

+ Put your baby on his back from birth.

+ Make sure your baby's face is uncovered when he sleeps.

+ Use a firm, clean mattress that fits snugly into the cot or bassinette.

+ The cot must meet Australian standards for cots.

+ You need to tuck the bedclothes in so they are not loose around the baby.

+ Place the baby's feet at the bottom of the cot when he is sleeping.

+ Keep quilts, doonas, duvets, pillows and cot bumpers out of the cot.

One of the major things parents worry about is whether their baby is too cold. I tell them that their baby feels the same temperature as they do — that is, if you feel cold then your baby will feel cold, if you are hot then your baby will likely be hot. Babies sleep better when it is cooler rather than too hot — they seem to struggle in the heat. Make sure the room is between about 18°C and 20°C and that the baby is dressed appropriately for the temperature and has bedding that will keep him warm but not hot. Keep the bedding to a bottom fitted sheet, a top sheet and a blanket. If your baby is wrapped well, you may not actually need the sheet in the warmer months. If it is winter, you can use a woollen blanket rather than a cotton blanket if you are worried about the temperature but it is really important not to overheat your baby.

## Wrapping or swaddling

I am a *huge* fan of the wrap! Young babies sleep more peacefully and for much longer if they are wrapped — and wrapped snugly. I teach all my parents my version of the wrap or swaddle, and it usually differs from what they have been taught in hospital. Most maternity hospitals teach parents to wrap their babies with their arms bent up so their hands are up near their mouths. I have tried a few versions over the years, including that one but I actually find it is better if you wrap your baby with his hands down by his sides.

I've provided instructions for my preferred wrapping technique on pages 50 and 51.

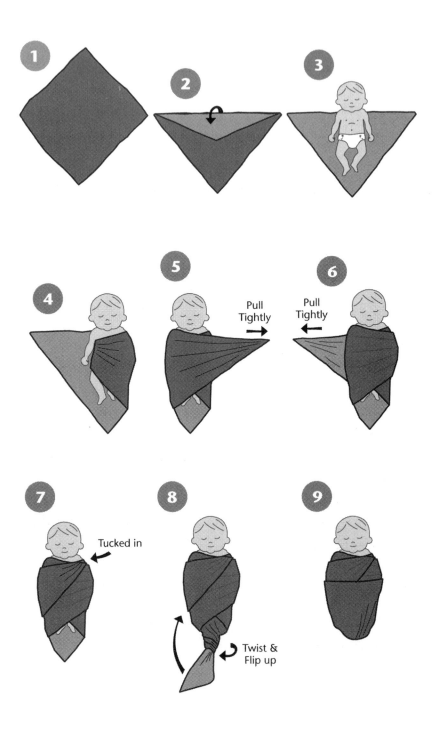

1   Place the wrap on a flat surface in a diamond shape.

2   Fold the top corner down so you have a straight line across the top.

3   Place the baby in the middle with her head above the fold. Baby's arms should be down by her side.

4   While holding the baby's left arm in close to her body, pull the right side of the wrap (your right-hand side, not the baby's) over and tuck it in firmly under the baby's body.

5   Make sure the top of the wrap comes up over baby's shoulder and pull firmly when wrapping over the other side of the baby's body.

6   Hold the baby's right arm in close to her body and wrap the left side (your left-hand side) over the baby while pulling firmly.

7   Wrap all the way around the baby's body (if you have a big wrap then tuck the end into the front of the wrap).

8   Twist the tail of the wrap up close to the baby's feet.

9   Bring the tail up the front of the baby's body and wrap it firmly around the baby.

Don't be afraid to wrap your baby really snugly. Babies are born with a startle reflex, called the Moro reflex. This reflex can be a response to a loud or unexpected noise or when the baby feels like he is falling, which can happen just as he is drifting off to sleep. When babies startle, their little arms will spread out wide and then come back in towards their body. They can also arch their backs when they startle, so they will often get a fright and may start to cry. If your baby is wrapped with his arms up near his face and not very snugly, this startle will have more of an effect: he can hit himself with his flailing arms, cry or just wake up rather than continue with his sleep. Wrapping your baby will limit the effect of this startle and that is why I prefer to wrap with the arms down. The choice, of course, is completely yours but I do recommend wrapping your baby this way. I have been to many homes where the baby has been unsettled and once I have wrapped them in this way, miraculously they sleep — and sleep, and sleep. Wrapping snugly can really be all that is needed to settle an unsettled baby.

## Sleep cycles

In the first few weeks of life new babies tend to sleep well, usually between feeds for anywhere between one-and-a-half and three hours at a time. You might have a baby that sleeps more than this at night, however, or less than this both day and night, and that is okay too.

New babies have shorter sleep cycles than adults and each cycle can last about 20 to 40 minutes. They also spend a lot of time in 'active sleep', or rapid eye movement (REM) sleep. You will notice that when you baby is asleep he might be squirming a bit, his eyes might flicker open occasionally and he might seem to be smiling or frowning and making strange noises. New babies fall into this 'active sleep' immediately after going to sleep so be aware that he is still asleep even if he is a bit noisy.

Very young babies also have no distinction between night and day and can wake regularly for feeding at any time. This changes at around six to eight weeks, when they start to distinguish between day and night and can start to sleep a bit longer at night and be more alert during the day.

By three months they should have settled into a definite night and day pattern of sleep, with more sleep at night and three separate sleeps during the day. By six months their sleep cycles will be more like an adult's and they should be able to sleep for nine to 12 hours overnight and have two sleeps during the day.

It is good to watch your baby when he is asleep so you can distinguish between his sleep cycles. If he is in 'active sleep' he can be quite noisy and squirmy. This doesn't mean he is ready to wake up and be fed. Often, after about 20 minutes of active sleep he will fall silent and be very still and calm and sound asleep. So you should wait until they are really awake before getting them up.

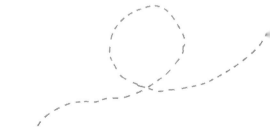

# Crying and settling

Crying is a very normal thing for a baby to do. The cry is designed to get attention, which is what you need to give your baby when she is crying. I am not a believer in letting a young baby cry on their own. A young baby will cry because something is not right and you need to attend to that. There is no way you can spoil a young baby with your attention — the baby needs you as she can't care for herself at all.

That said, sometimes a baby will cry and there will be nothing you can find that is wrong. This can be very distressing and frustrating for you. Remember that your baby will be picking up on your mood, so remain calm and just hold your baby and she should eventually calm down.

*Never shake your baby. If you are feeling frustrated and angry with him, put your baby down somewhere safe and leave the room for a minute or two until you feel more able to cope with his crying. If there are other people in the house, ask them to take over for you or call someone and ask them to come over and help you.

Crying does change as the baby gets older but at this early stage there are usually a few reasons why your baby will be crying:

✦ *Hunger.* If your baby hasn't been fed for a couple of hours or more, then this would be the most likely reason for the crying. Young babies need to be fed regularly and so even if he has had a recent feed you could try to top him up with a bit more milk to see if that calms him.

✦ *Tiredness.* Young babies should only be awake for an hour at a time and so she might be telling you that she needs to go to sleep. Overtired babies can cry a lot and very intensely so it is always a good idea to get your baby to sleep *before* she gets overtired.

✦ *Wet or dirty.* Babies usually don't like to sleep with a dirty or very wet nappy, so always check that his nappy is clean if he is unhappy.

✦ *Wind.* Most babies need to be burped or winded after they have fed. Keep your baby upright for five to ten minutes after a feed to get all the wind up. If she has a sore tummy, you can put her up over your shoulder with her tummy pressed against your shoulder or lay her across your legs with her tummy against your thighs. Sometimes gentle pressure on her stomach can relieve pain, and cycling her legs while lying on her back can help with lower wind.

✦ *Too hot/too cold.* Always check whether your baby is comfortable when you put him down to sleep. Babies don't like it if they are too hot or too cold.

- *Illness.* As per the section on page 39, if your baby has been crying for extended periods and there is nothing you can do to settle her, she might be unwell. Seek medical advice in this case.

- *She needs a cuddle.* Very young babies sometimes need to be held to settle them, as they need contact with their parents. Pick her up and give her a cuddle if you think it will help.

Walking while holding the baby, or rocking, swinging or bouncing can also help calm a crying baby. Sometimes sucking can help too so you can feed them, or offer a dummy (after the baby is over two weeks old) or a finger to suck on.

I also find that a nice soothing bath is a great way to settle a crying baby. He might cry once you have taken him out of the nice warm bath but then feeding him after that should calm him down.

Never leave a young baby to cry on her own for more than a minute. A young baby needs your attention.

## Babybliss Technique

Over my years of dealing with babies and primarily with their sleep issues, I have developed my own philosophy on how you can get your baby to be a great sleeper so you can enjoy the early years without you or your baby having to go through too much stress. Obviously there will be hiccups along the way and times when you feel you have no idea what is going on. The Babybliss Settling Technique and the Babybliss philosophy give you something to fall back on during these times and guide you through your baby's young life.

I believe that if you get those early days sorted then the rest will fall into place. You really don't want to have a four-year-old child who is still not sleeping through the night — and that can happen!

I don't believe in strict and rigid routines while your baby is a newborn. Those very strict, clock-watching routines can set you up to fail and lead to feelings of frustration and depression. It is almost impossible to get a newborn baby to stay awake for more than an hour and a lot of those routines have your baby awake for up to three hours at a time. They also encourage you to wake your sleeping newborn after only short naps, which is another thing I disagree with.

The Babybliss Technique is all about getting to know your baby in those early days and letting the baby set the pace with regard to feeding and sleeping. That said, you can definitely have a plan but rather than looking at the whole day, you should focus on each cycle of feeding, activity and sleep. These cycles can be anywhere between two and four hours long with a newborn, but you need to feed your baby when she is hungry. This shorter pattern will set up your milk supply, and also means that your baby should settle and sleep well until she needs to be fed again.

You should keep a log (see page 107) to help you start to see patterns emerge with your baby. Some babies will sleep more in the morning and be more wakeful in the evenings; some babies will need to be fed more frequently in the evening and so on. Keeping a log helps you to get to know your baby better.

As your baby grows you can begin to have more of a structure to your days and nights, and by three months you should have a definite routine for your baby. That said, I am not a fan of being completely rigid with any routine but by this time you should have your baby sleeping in one to two large chunks at night and having three definite sleeps during the day.

The best thing about the Babybliss Technique is that it offers parents an effective way of teaching babies to be good sleepers without having to resort to stressful techniques such as controlled crying. But it also means that you won't have to continue feeding your baby during the night until she is two and you won't have to have your baby in the bed with you if you don't want to. The Babybliss Technique is a gentle way to get your baby to learn to self-settle when he is able and to work towards having a great sleeping child, who is happy and secure in his bed at night.

## Baby routines

It is really important for children to have routine and ritual in their days. Structure and routine make children less anxious and if they know what to expect they tend to be more cooperative. It allows them to have a sense of control over their world, a world that is essentially out of their control and scary at times.

Routine gives the day a rhythm, and this rhythm becomes familiar if it is repeated the same way every day. If you have a routine your child will become aware of the structure of the day and know what to expect and what is expected of them. Children with routines can be confident and secure little people as they are aware of what each day will hold. The routine and the rituals that go along with the day mean they are certain that every evening dinner is followed by a bath, then a story from Dad, and then it is time for bed. When a child has no routine they are unsure of what each day will hold. They don't know when they will get fed or when they are supposed to sleep and so they can become quite clingy and unsure of themselves.

Routine and ritual also give parents the confidence to know what is happening from one moment to the next, which can be tricky when you have a new baby. As your baby grows it is really nice to know that he will be asleep at certain times of the day and be awake at other times. This certainty means you can plan activities, outings and visitors. Many times I have been to homes where there is no routine and the mother tells me she isn't a 'routine person'. After I explain that having a routine doesn't mean that she has to stick to it to the minute but it will mean that her baby will be happier and she will be able to plan when she can go to the supermarket and so on, she usually starts to be more of a 'routine person'. And then once she puts the routine in place there can be an amazing transformation in her child. Things all of a sudden seem to work better. There is less crying and resistance from the child and the day runs more smoothly.

Babies and children *love* routine. This is a fact!

With brand-new babies the routine and ritual is around feeding and sleeping. In the early weeks your baby will develop a basic eating and sleeping routine, but you don't need to rigidly watch the clock. The most important things to remember are that your baby should only be awake for about an hour at a time and that he should sleep between feeds.

The problem I most often observe in parents with small babies is that the baby doesn't want to sleep during the day and is really difficult to settle. All new babies require a lot of sleep, about 16 to 18 hours a day. Although your baby may look like he doesn't want to sleep, he really *needs* to sleep, and it is up to you to teach him how. A new baby is pretty much a blank canvas when he is born and he needs to learn how to do everything in his life, including sleeping. You are your baby's teacher and you need to teach him this skill, as well as many other things throughout his life.

As a general rule, your baby should be fed every three to four hours. If your baby is breastfed or experiencing a growth spurt, he may need feeding as often as every two hours. Growth spurts usually occur every three weeks and last for 24 to 48 hours.

New mothers should keep a logbook and write down every time the baby sleeps or eats and wets or dirties his nappy. There is an example of a log on page 107. This will help you keep track of your baby's routine and give you an idea of how long the baby is sleeping and how long a feed takes. It's also a handy way to get used to the noises a baby makes and what they mean. For example, if your baby is starting to whinge or become unsettled after being awake for two hours, it means he is tired and needs to sleep.

It's important to weigh your baby regularly to monitor how much weight he is gaining. With breastfed babies it's difficult to know exactly how much milk your baby is drinking each feed, so weighing him every week or two can give you a good idea of whether he is drinking enough or not.

If your baby isn't putting on weight, he may not be getting enough to eat. Newborns need to have at least 20 minutes of constant sucking each time they feed to get enough milk for their growth. This may take up to an hour to achieve when they are tiny, as newborns often fall asleep while feeding — it's a tiring job for them! If this happens then wake your baby, which you can do by changing his nappy or burping him.

Burping is something all babies need the chance to do. Not all babies burp after a feed, but you need to let them try to burp. The best way to burp a baby is to just sit him upright on your lap with one hand placed under his chin and the other supporting his back. You don't need to rub or pat; the wind should come up of its own accord. If there is no burp after a couple of minutes, you can continue with the feed. If you feel your baby isn't feeding enough or putting on enough weight, you should consult your doctor.

If your baby is only sleeping for short, unscheduled periods there are a few things you may need to consider. These will be discussed in detail on pages 103–104.

## Managing twins or more

Caring for one newborn baby can be exhausting, but caring for two or more is completely overwhelming. To make things easier and to help you maintain your sanity, your parenting routine will need to be far more structured. For example, you should try to keep both babies on the same schedule; if one wakes and is ready to feed while the other is still asleep, you should wake the other so they can feed at the same time then go to sleep together. If one wakes and they are not due to be fed then you should try to get them back to sleep until the feed is due.

This routine should be followed regardless of whether the babies are breastfed or bottle-fed. Feeding two babies at once on a bottle can be a difficult task, however, especially as newborns can't sit upright to feed, so you will need extra help. With multiple births in particular, it's essential to have someone else with you as much as possible in the early weeks, whether it's your partner or a friend or family member. AMBA (www.amba.org.au) can also give you advice on finding support in your local area.

# Chapter 3

# Confident parenting

Babies may look tiny and fragile, and in many respects they are, but they are also incredibly resilient and robust. You don't need to be afraid of your baby, she is not that scary.

You have to set the tone and lead the way with your baby — you are her primary carer and educator, you need to show her how to be in this world, so take charge and do just that. You are her role model — the most important role you will play in your life. I hear a lot of comments from parents like, 'My baby doesn't like that' or 'My baby doesn't like to sleep during the day' or 'My baby just won't do what I want her to do'. But you are the parent and as the parent if you want your baby to fit into a certain routine or do something that is within her capabilities, then you need to teach her how to do that.

A baby won't get the hang of something if you give up after one try. I don't know anyone who can get the hang of how to do something by being shown just once. The keys to teaching a baby something new are repetition and consistency. You need to repeat the process over and over again, and do it the same way every time. That way it will start to become familiar to your baby and she will recognise what is happening. Then she will take it on as her own.

# Watching, listening to and understanding your baby

When you bring a new baby home it can be very daunting and scary, especially if you haven't had much experience with small babies. The most overlooked piece of advice given to parents is that you really need to get to know your baby. She is a new little person in your life and your family, she has a personality type, with her own little idiosyncrasies and likes and dislikes. So it is very important to get to know your new baby, just like you would a new friend. The way you do this is to watch her closely, observe and listen to the way she behaves and reacts to things, listen to the way she cries and just generally getting a sense of who she is — even though she is tiny.

For example, if your baby has a particular way of crying, whether a real bellow or a sound more like a little bird, this is just your baby's cry. Sometimes when I visit parents they tell me that their baby sounds like she is being tortured when she cries or she sounds like she is in real pain and it is very distressing to the parents. And, of course, it is distressing to hear your baby sound like she is in pain. First and foremost, you need to ascertain that there is nothing physically wrong with your baby, then you need to get used to the way she sounds. And yes, I have heard some babies really scream the place down, and they wind up in no time at all. At the other end of the scale are the babies who just sound like they are having a whinge, they never seem to work up to a big wail.

The type of cry doesn't mean that one of these babies is more distressed than the other, this is just who they are and the way they behave. Another thing to notice about your baby is how she deals with going off to sleep. Is your baby a baby who winds down to sleep by having a little cry or a little squeal? Often with new babies they have all this amazing amount of stimulation going on all the time, and when they go off to sleep they just need to expel that pent-up energy by having a big yell to wind themselves down. This is a normal thing, not a bad thing. However, I think you should not leave your baby on her own while she is having a bit of a yell. Just stand beside her with your hand on her. You can gently pat her if you like, but just notice that this is what she does every time she goes off to sleep and so it is okay.

If this is what your baby does you need to acknowledge that this is simply her and you won't get distressed every time it happens or wonder why she cries every time you put her down to sleep. Other babies might just turn their head to the side, have a bit of a stare off into the distance, a couple of little squirms and then go off to sleep. Therefore, as a new parent take time to watch your baby, watch how she behaves, watch how she goes off to sleep, watch how she responds to stimulation around her. Be very aware of who she is and really get to know her just like she has to get to know you, because knowing your baby is an important start in the process of understanding why she might do certain things sometimes.

Babies naturally develop their own rituals and routines. For example, she might turn her head to the side when you start to wrap her, she might fight the wrap for a bit once she is wrapped, then relax and go to sleep. These are all things you need to notice that can help you to understand your baby and read her behaviour.

# Using your instincts

By watching and understanding and getting to know your baby, you can use your instinct in dealing with her, which can really help both you and your baby. These days new parents can find it really difficult to tap into their parental instinct because there is such an overload of information available to them, whether from books, friends or family members. They all tell you different things and offer different opinions and techniques on how to deal with your baby. Mothers, particularly, have a really strong parental instinct, you just need to allow yourself to tap into it and go with it.

We have all heard stories about mothers who were told by a health professional that there was nothing wrong with their child but deep down they knew there was something very wrong and they followed that instinct for the best. If something doesn't feel right then don't do it, or if you have an urge to try something that is opposite to what someone told you to do because you think your baby will respond to it, then go with it. More often than not you will find that it works. That is how I teach babies to sleep or settle or do things I want them to do, I watch them and see how they respond to me, trust my instinct and go with it. And although I am not related to any of the babies I work with, using my instinct still works. So imagine how powerful your instinct, as your baby's mother or father, can be.

As parents you will all have some parental instinct about your child. I think mothers have a stronger instinct than fathers most of the time simply because they have carried this child within them for 40 weeks. As parents you need to really try to tap into this instinct and use it to learn about and deal with your baby.

There is so much information available on parenting and babies that to some extent we have lost the ability to listen to our gut feelings. We often second-guess ourselves with thoughts such as 'But the book doesn't say that' or 'Louise said she did something different and it worked with her baby', and so on. The most powerful relationship you will have is the one between you and your child, and you will know this little person better than anyone else who comes into their life — especially now, while she is a baby. So you should really take the time to get to know your baby. Study her and get to know her likes and dislikes and her little idiosyncrasies. We all have them and so does your baby. This way you can tailor the way you deal with your baby to suit her as a little individual.

# Routine and ritual

Routine and ritual is a great thing for both your baby and you. Having some routine and ritual, especially in the early days, will help you to develop your parenting confidence. You will start to know your baby and how he responds to the day.

In the early days the routine should be fairly fluid. You will know that your baby feeds for a certain length of time, then you go through the rituals of burping, wrapping and settling, and then he sleeps for a certain length of time. This gives you something to do the same way every time, and as you get more familiar and confident with the process, so does your baby.

# Enjoying your baby

New parents can get so caught up in trying to get everything 'right' with their baby that they forget to enjoy the whole experience. While the lead-up to having a baby can be an anxious but also very exciting time, once the baby is born you can get so caught up in your head with all the parenting information and trying to fit all the things in you are 'supposed' to be doing that you completely forget you have this amazing little person in your life.

The experience of having a new baby is full of joy and love and amazement. Watching a new baby develop and grow is a wonder. You need to stop and watch. No-one really knows what they are doing when they become first-time parents. It takes time to work out how to deal with every day, so give yourself a break, sit back and go with it a bit. Remember, you will never get these early days back, and they really should be special, enjoyable times.

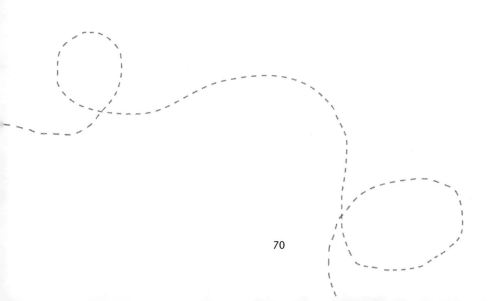

# Chapter 4

# Your newborn baby: the first six weeks

# Baby sleeping

In the first couple of weeks of your new baby's life, he might be sleeping really well and you are thinking, 'I don't know what everyone was on about, this is a breeze!' Well, I hate to rain on your parade but a lot of newborns can be sleepy in the first week or so of their lives. Newborns usually feed and then sleep and don't do much else.

There are some babies though, who from the minute they are born are very keen to get on with their life. They are alert, seeming to take in everything around them and are usually not too keen on sleeping when they are supposed to — or when you think they are supposed to. But generally, most newborns *need* to sleep, regardless of whether they want to or not. A newborn baby needs about 16 to 18 hours of sleep in a 24-hour period and some babies can have more than that. The most important thing to understand, however, is that most babies need to be *taught* how to be great sleepers. If there is one thing that all parents should be told before they have children, I would love it to be that.

Just like everything in your baby's life, sleep is a skill they need to learn, and as their parents and principal educators you have to be the ones to teach them how to sleep. So be prepared for that, and you really need to start from day one.

Start out as you mean to continue: if you want your baby to sleep in his own cot and be able to put himself to sleep, then you need to start out with that in mind. It is also very important, however, to know that newborn babies are not able to self-settle. They usually can't do this until they are about 12 weeks old. But with that in mind you can still employ settling techniques that encourage your little baby to learn to put himself to sleep.

## When should my baby sleep, and for how long?

Newborn babies need a lot of sleep. This is a really important thing to know about newborn babies. An equally important thing to know is that sleep promotes sleep. It is a complete fallacy that if you keep a baby awake or limit the amount of sleep he has during the day he will then sleep better at night. In fact, the opposite is true.

I deal with many small babies who don't get enough sleep during the day and then are awake all night and this will only get worse as they grow because they don't know how to sleep. A baby who sleeps well during the day will often be a great sleeper overnight, and he will carry this skill with him as he grows.

As I've mentioned earlier, a newborn baby should only be awake for about an hour at a time. I know a lot of you will be thinking that this is complete rubbish because your baby can stay awake for longer than that. But in my experience a newborn baby can only take about 60 minutes of stimulation and activity before he gets tired and needs to sleep again. This is another one of those facts that new parents should be told before they have the baby!

If you think about it, a newborn baby has come out of a contained and peaceful place and been thrust into the hustle and bustle of our world. His little brain is trying to take in everything he sees, hears, touches, smells and feels, and make sense of it. All this is stimulating him, constantly. And so I recommend that for the first six weeks of your baby's life you limit the amount of activity you do outside the house.

Your baby needs to get used to being in the world and the most important place for him is his home. This is where he will spend most of his time, this is where he will sleep and so this is where he needs to feel most secure. If you are taking your baby out all day, every day, he has no opportunity to get used to being in his home. He will be constantly stimulated by noises and sights and will be very unsettled most of the time and find it difficult to sleep when he is supposed to.

I often hear from parents that their baby sleeps well when he is in the pram or in the car but when I ask more questions about how he is when they get home and how he settles when he is supposed to, they tell me that the baby has difficulty settling. Babies take in stimulation whether they are awake or asleep, and so when you are out all day with your baby in the pram, even if he is asleep, he is still absorbing the noises around him and being stimulated. That is why I teach parents to monitor the amount of stimulation a baby is getting because this will affect how he sleeps. This also includes stimulation at home.

Finally bringing your new baby home is very exciting and you will have many visitors wanting to catch a glimpse of the new addition but I recommend that, at least for the first two weeks, you limit the amount of visitors to your home. This is not just for the baby but for the parents as well, especially the mum. You need to have as much rest as you can in those first few weeks after having a baby — there is a reason why in some countries women don't leave the home for a month after they have a baby!

## Be patient!

One of the things that many new parents don't realise is that you need to be patient and calm when dealing with a newborn baby. I can understand that at first a lot of parents are eager to get through the day and get the baby to bed so they can actually have some time to themselves. And that is a great thing to work towards, but a newborn baby needs plenty of time to learn about her world and adjust to all the things that are happening to her.

Therefore, when it comes to feeding and especially settling a baby, don't rush her. Give her time to understand or adjust to what you are doing. Don't rush through the feeding — it can take up to an hour to feed a newborn — and don't rush the burping. Give her at least five minutes after the feed to be upright and, most importantly, don't rush the settling before you put her into her cot. A new baby needs to be wound down, to get past what she has absorbed over the last 60 minutes, and calm down enough to be ready to close her eyes and drift off to sleep.

A baby picks up on your cues too. If you are rushing or anxious to get through to the next stage of the day, she will feel that and more often than not get stressed and anxious herself, which will lead her to being much more difficult to settle than she normally might be.

You both need time together and this is a wonderful, amazing bonding time that you can spend getting to know each other. Be patient, take a deep breath and relax into each part of the day.

## Babybliss routine and ritual

I cannot emphasise enough how important it is for children to have routine and ritual in their days. Structure and routine make children less anxious and, if they know what to expect, they become more cooperative.

A routine can start from the day your child is born, but it is near impossible to get a newborn baby into a routine based on doing things at the same time every day. With that in mind, start a routine that is not too focused on times of the day, such as waking your baby at 9 am and keeping him up till 10.30 am and then putting him down to sleep till 11.30 am etc. These kinds of routines are stressful for the mother and the newborn baby, and are not necessarily conducive to the regularity of the mother's milk supply or for teaching a baby to be a great sleeper. A Babybliss newborn routine is more about each feed, activity, sleep cycle and with a newborn these cycles occur about every three to four hours, but can be closer to two hours if your baby is having a growth spurt.

The activity part of the routine involves the nappy change, the cuddle, the burping and a little chat, not much else at this early stage. The focus of the routine is that new babies can only be awake for approximately one hour. After this length of time they will start to get overtired and overstimulated, making the sleeping part of the cycle more difficult and then throwing everything out. So while it is sensible to watch for tired signs it is also wise to keep one eye on the clock. When that hour is drawing to a close, make sure you are on your way to getting the baby into bed.

Tired signs for newborn babies are:

+ grizzling or crying
+ increasing jerky arm and leg movements
+ staring into space without blinking
+ clenching of fists
+ grimacing
+ yawning.

If you see your baby yawn and she has been fed and awake for close to an hour, then it is time to prepare her for sleep. Wrap her up and get her into bed before the next yawn if you can.

At this age a baby should be sleeping for two to three hours between feeds and be averaging five to six sleeps in a 24-hour period.

The routine for a newborn baby would go something like:

1. baby wakes up
2. feed (breast or bottle)

3.  activity — in the middle of the feed have some activity like the nappy change

4.  feed — finish off the feed, and in some cases the feed will take the whole hour

5.  more activity — burp baby, wrap baby up, comforting pat, some soothing words or a soft song

6.  sleep — back into bed.

Remember that it is okay to put your baby down if she is awake, in fact as she gets older this is preferable. You want to be teaching your baby how to put herself to sleep with minimum assistance from you so as she grows she won't need to be fed, rocked or patted off to sleep. Some parents are terrified of their baby not being sound asleep by the time they are put into the cot. But it is absolutely okay to put your baby down to sleep with her eyes open. If she is calm then you can walk away and let her try to go off to sleep without any help from you. This is a great start to teaching her how to self-settle.

## Sleeping problems

One of the things I hear quite regularly from parents is that their baby doesn't like to sleep, especially during the day or in the early evening. The thing to remember is that your little baby really doesn't know what she likes or wants, or needs for that matter. That is something you, as her parents, need to teach her. So although your baby appears to not want to sleep, sleep is really what she needs.

By the time a baby is three weeks old she will have really woken up and discovered her voice and her ability to cry. This is often around the time that I get calls from desperate parents wanting me to give them advice on how to get their baby to sleep. Their newborn baby was sleeping with no problem at all and now it seems that all she wants to do is stay awake. This behaviour is very normal. Most newborn babies are quite drowsy for the first weeks and sleep well between feeds. Then something changes, they become more alert to their surroundings and can start to have more and more difficulty falling asleep when they are supposed to. Often, to combat that, parents resort to all sorts of things to get their baby to sleep.

This can be a tricky time as a lot of babies start to catnap — that is, they sleep for only one sleep cycle, which can be 30 to 45 minutes. They can also start to be unsettled after their feed and difficult to get off to sleep. The thing to remember at this time is that the behaviour will pass but this is when you really need to put on your teacher's hat and teach her how to be a great sleeper.

For example, your baby has been fed, she has been awake for about 60 minutes and she is showing tired signs and so you know it is time for her to go to sleep. You wrap her up and place her in her bed, she looks drowsy but as soon as you put her down she starts to squirm, her eyes ping open and then she starts to cry. What do you do?

The thing to do is go one step back: you need to prepare your baby for sleep *before* she goes into her bed. Once she has been wrapped, give her some wind-down time. This can take up to 20 minutes. After burping her (which we will discuss on page 101) and wrapping her up nice and snug, pick her up and either cradle her in your arms or hold her upright under your chin or up on your shoulder. You then need to pat her, quite firmly on her nappy or on her back, up high near her shoulders, in a rhythmical manner, at the pace of a heartbeat. You can stand still or you can walk around the room while you are doing this, whatever seems most comfortable, and continue patting her until all her squirming has stopped and her little eyes are staring into space or starting to close. Then very calmly place her in her bed and put one hand on her chest and the other hand on her legs and just keep your hands there until you feel comfortable to leave her to go off to sleep.

Don't be afraid if your baby has her eyes open when you leave. This is not a bad thing. In fact, it is ideal to let the baby do the last little bit of putting herself to sleep if she can. If once you put her down into bed she starts to squirm again or opens her eyes, don't pick her up but just gently pat her, again rhythmically in the pace of a heartbeat, on her shoulder or her arm. You need to do this until she is in the sleep zone — that is, her eyes are staring off into space, or are partly or fully closed.

Keep going in to her room and patting her until she has gone to sleep. You may need to spend longer with her each time you return to help her to actually go off to sleep because the longer she is awake the more overtired she will become, so you don't want the settling to go on for too long.

## *My baby still won't sleep!*

If a baby is overtired, or overstimulated — that is, she has been awake for more than 90 minutes or has had a busy day out in the car or the pram or had loads of people wanting to hold her or look at her or gurgle at her — then she will be unlikely to go to sleep in this way. An overtired baby can be really distressed. She will cry until she is red in the face, she can pull her legs up and generally behave like she could be in pain. The cry is pretty distinct, though. It starts off like a fuss then builds to a full-on scream — a 'waa waaaa waaaaaa' scream. You will notice this cry comes in cycles, and she can have three to four of these cycles. So she will fuss, build to the cry — 'waa, waa, waaaa' — then stop, then start to fuss again, build to the cry and then stop and so on.

An overtired baby finds it really difficult to get into a deep sleep. She is so 'wired' that she spends a lot of time in active or REM sleep and is unable to drop down into her deeper sleep. When a baby is like this there is pretty much only one way to get her to go to sleep and stay asleep for a decent amount of time.

If your baby is overtired, you need to prolong the settling that you do before you put her into bed. Do exactly as you would normally do if you were preparing her for bed. Then take her into a quiet, darkened room because a lot of the squirming and crying she is doing is because she wants to block out the world and go to sleep. Pat her quite firmly while walking around the room; you can jiggle her too and shush or hum to her until she is asleep. This may take a while and you may have to live through a couple of screaming cycles, but be assured that she *will* eventually go to sleep. You need to remain calm and stick with the settling technique you are using, because if you think she isn't settling and you try something else, like putting her in the pram and taking her for a walk, you will just add to her overstimulation and compound the problem. So be patient, she will go to sleep.

Once she has closed her eyes, instead of putting her immediately into her cot as you would normally do, continue to hold her until she gets through all her active sleep and drops into a deep sleep. If you try to put her down while she is still making faces and her eyes are fluttering then be assured her little eyes will ping open the moment she hits that mattress.

You may have to hold her for 15 to 20 minutes. You will know when she is in a deep sleep because she will stop making faces, she will be still and heavy in your arms, her little face will go pale and she may get dark circles under her eyes. Always test whether she is deeply asleep by gently moving the baby away from your body, like you are going to put her down. If she stays still and asleep then you can be pretty sure you can put her into the cot without her waking up.

In short, this is how you get an overtired baby to sleep:

✦ make sure she has a full tummy
✦ burp her
✦ wrap her nice and snugly
✦ take her into a darkened room
✦ cradle her in your arms or on your shoulder and pat her firmly and rhythmically while she goes through three or four crying cycles

◆ stay calm if she continues to cry

◆ be consistent and maintain your settling technique —
changing it will only make her worse

◆ once she has stopped crying continue to hold her until she is
in a deep sleep

◆ be confident with your settling technique — your baby will
pick up on your anxiety and respond to that.

## CASE STUDY
## Lily

When I first met Lily's parents they looked like they hadn't slept for weeks, which was in fact the case. Lily was six weeks old and she hadn't slept for more than about 40 minutes at a time. If someone was holding her she could sleep for about an hour but this was just becoming impractical as she grew bigger and her parents became more and more exhausted.

When they had Lily, her parents had no idea that young babies should be awake for only an hour at a time. They thought, like many other new parents, that Lily would happily go off to sleep when she was tired and stay asleep until she was due to be fed again.

I could tell that Lily was completely overtired. She looked tired and had dark circles under her little eyes. Her mum demonstrated how they were trying to get her to sleep, the wrapping and the settling. Because Lily really hadn't slept for six weeks there was no way that she was going to be able to go off to sleep and stay that way unless we got her into her deep sleep *before* putting her into her cot.

Firstly, I made sure that Lily had a big feed. Often overtired babies don't drink enough because they are so tired they fall asleep while feeding. Then I demonstrated how to wrap Lily so she couldn't get her arms out, because overtired babies can be very jerky and squirmy so they need to feel contained when going off to sleep. Then I asked Lily's dad to hold her in his arms and pat her off to sleep. Once she was asleep I made sure that he kept holding her until she had gone through all her active sleep. Then we put her down in her cot, tucked her in firmly and left her.

Miraculously, she slept for over two hours, something she had never done before. Now that she was less overtired I decided that we should keep her awake-time very limited for the next 24 hours, until she had caught up on sleep and was not overtired any more. We got her up, fed her and then put her straight back to bed. Her total up-time was about 45 minutes. This time she went quickly to sleep and we could put her down in her cot before she was in her deep sleep. After a bit of patting in the cot she went off to sleep with not too much resistance and again slept for two hours.

Lily's parents continued this routine for the next 24 hours, each time finding it easier to get her off to sleep. Apart from the odd time where she woke before she was meant to and needed to be resettled, she pretty much stuck to the routine.

After the 24 hours Lily was a different baby. The dark circles were gone and she was engaging much more with her parents. They could then keep her up for the whole hour and have her go off to sleep *before* she got too tired.

## Is it okay to use a dummy?

I do encourage the use of dummies in some young babies, much to the horror of other health professionals I am sure! I have found that if you have a baby that is particularly 'sucky' — that is, she really likes to suck to put herself to sleep or to calm herself — introducing a dummy can save you from having a baby attached to you all day. A dummy can also help the baby get to sleep without too much fuss and also go back to sleep if she wakes before she is meant to.

I do think it is best though, if you are breastfeeding your baby, to wait until you have established your feeding before you introduce a dummy (because there can be some risk of your baby getting confused between the dummy and the nipple). This usually takes about two weeks after the birth. And then only use the dummy when you are having settling problems. Don't force the dummy on your baby at every sleep because she usually won't need it every time she goes to sleep.

It will take some practice for a baby to accept a dummy because it is a different way of sucking, if she is breastfed. So you will need to gently hold it in her mouth until she starts to suck.

Once she has the hang of it then she will suck away until she has calmed herself down and is ready to go off to sleep. At this stage a baby will usually then spit the dummy out and go to sleep. Don't try to put the dummy back in; let her do that last bit of going off to sleep without it.

The drawback with using a dummy is that if you use it regularly for some months then the baby will become addicted to the sucking to go off to sleep. She will stop spitting it out and actually need it to go to sleep and stay asleep. My advice is that if you don't have to use one then don't, but if you do use a dummy try to get rid of it by the time your baby is four to five months old. By this age she will not be too addicted to it and you should be able to get rid of it without too much fuss.

## Sleeping summary

When you have a newborn, sleeping is all important and you will find that you are very focused on getting your baby to sleep. Sleep *is* really important for your baby, so if you are struggling, then following a few simple guidelines can help get you and your baby back on track.

Here are the most important things to remember about getting your baby to sleep well:

+ Be patient!
+ Your newborn baby needs to be awake for only 60 minutes at a time.
+ Sleep and food are very closely related — make sure your baby has a nice full tummy before trying to put her to bed.

✦ Your baby needs to sleep between feeds so if she is awake for an hour and is being fed every three hours, then she needs to be asleep for two hours.

✦ Keep outings to a minimum in the early days. Your baby needs to get used to her home and her parents before taking on the world.

✦ Wrap your baby snugly with her arms down before you put her to bed.

✦ Watch for tired signs and act upon them.

✦ If you have started with a settling technique, continue with it until it works — don't change in the middle.

✦ Start having a ritual around putting your baby to bed and continue that ritual as she grows.

## Settling summary

Sleep and settling go hand in hand but there is a process to settling your baby *before* they go to sleep. I believe that a young baby really needs to be well settled before they are put down to sleep. Once you have settled your baby well they should go off to sleep with little fuss.

Some tips on how to settle your baby effectively are:

✦ Make sure she has a full tummy.

✦ Hold her upright to allow her to burp for at least five minutes after the feed.

✦ Wrap her nice and snugly.

✦ Put her up over your shoulder or under your chin and pat her for a couple of minutes until she is calm.

✦ Be patient! If she is taking a while to calm just stick with it.

✦ When she is calm and drowsy, put her in her cot or bassinette.

✦ Keep your hands on her for a minute or two once she is down.

✦ Leave her to go off to sleep, if she isn't already. If you need to go back to her then pat her on her arm or shoulder gently until she is calm or asleep, then leave again.

✦ Be confident with your settling — your baby will know if you are anxious or panicked and respond to that.

## Baby feeding

Feeding is obviously a very important part of your baby's life. Babies feed to survive, develop and grow. Feeding a newborn can seem challenging and whether you are breastfeeding or bottle-feeding your baby, you both need to learn how to do it.

Breastfeeding is the preferred way of feeding a baby. There is plenty of research and literature available which attests that breast is best. That said, I am not in the business of making mothers feel guilty about not breastfeeding their babies. As long as the mother has been educated about the benefits of breast versus bottle and she makes a decision not to breastfeed, I think she needs to be supported in that decision.

Then there are those women who just can't make breastfeeding work. This can be incredibly frustrating and disappointing to a woman who has planned on breastfeeding her baby. If this is your situation then I would suggest that you seek as much help and advice as you can — and there are plenty of places to do that, such as your local baby health clinic, GP, paediatrician, or a private lactation consultant. If you decide to switch to bottle-feeding, or you have to switch to bottle-feeding, you absolutely deserve to be supported in that decision and again not be made to feel guilty about that — because, believe me, I am sure that you are already feeling guilty about something. As all mothers will know, the guilt factor kicks in as soon as that little person enters the world!

## Breastfeeding

Breastfeeding is a learnt skill, for you and your baby. A common thing I hear from new mothers is that they are surprised at how difficult breastfeeding is initially. Breastfeeding is one of those things that you can't imagine what it will be like until you are actually doing it — like childbirth, I guess. So as much as you read about it beforehand, which I really encourage you to do, you have to be actually doing it before you can grasp what it is like.

By the time you get home from hospital your milk should have come in, and hopefully you and your baby will be sorting out the attachment and building a routine around the feeding. Although at first you might not think breastfeeding your baby is a wonderful thing, if you stick with it you will find that it is a really lovely experience for you and your baby. Not to mention the convenience!

Some babies attach to the breast with little or no trouble at all and just get on with it from day one. Others take a bit longer to get going. Small babies with little mouths often have a bit of trouble attaching at first but this will improve with practice. The key is to really try to stick with it, get as much help as you need and over time you will get the hang of it and it will become a really natural process for you both.

### How to position your baby for feeding

Hopefully you had a good demonstration of how to get your baby on the breast while you were in hospital, but unfortunately quite a few new mothers get home and their attachment is still not great. There are a few things that can determine if your baby is positioned correctly on the breast:

- It doesn't hurt. At first you might have some pain when you initially attach your baby but this pain should subside altogether after about 20 sucks.
- Your baby has a good mouthful of breast. Make sure the baby has a lot of your areola as well as the nipple.
- Your baby's lips are slightly curled back. This indicates that she has a large amount of breast in her mouth.
- Your baby's chin is well in against your breast.
- Your baby's chest is against your chest.
- You can hear your baby swallow. The swallow can be a very small sound or an obvious gulp. The swallow means she is attached correctly and drinking the milk.

## *Problems and solutions*

Some women and babies breastfeed easily from day one and never really have a problem. But others can find it challenging and really struggle in the early days to get it working well. If you are struggling, remember that you are not alone. Breastfeeding can take a lot of practice and so I encourage you to seek professional advice or talk to other breastfeeding mothers if you are having difficulties. But persevere for as long as you can, because it can take quite a few weeks to get the breastfeeding really sorted and comfortable. If you are really struggling with it then the ABA or a private lactation consultant can be a great help.

Some common difficulties or problems that women may encounter with breastfeeding are discussed in the following pages.

## — Not enough milk

Not having enough milk, or the fear of not having enough milk, is one of the major reasons why women give up breastfeeding their babies. According to the ABA, nearly all mothers are capable of producing enough milk to feed their baby.

The signs that you do have enough milk include:

✦ your baby having about six to eight wet nappies every 24 hours

✦ if your baby is very young then he might be dirtying his nappy every feed or every second feed

✦ your baby's poos are soft and smooth

✦ your baby's skin colour is good and he has good muscle tone

✦ when your baby is awake he is alert and not always wanting to be feeding

✦ your baby is gaining weight and growing in length.

When looking at your baby's weight, you need to take genetics into consideration. If you and your partner are not very big people then it is likely that you are not going to have a very big baby. As long as your baby is consistently gaining weight then everything is good.

There are things that can affect how much milk your baby is getting at each feed, such as the way he is positioned on the breast and, primarily, the attachment. Make sure both these things are working so that the baby is able to get the milk easily. If you really feel like you don't have enough milk then you can try to increase your supply by feeding your baby more regularly. Try to feed every two hours for 24 to 48 hours. You also need to make sure that the baby is emptying the first breast before you swap to the other side. Swapping too soon can mean that your brain is getting the message that it doesn't need to make so much milk and will reduce your supply.

There are also medications you can take and natural remedies, such as herbal teas, to increase your milk supply. But if you are really concerned, get some advice from a lactation consultation, the ABA or your GP.

## — Too much milk or engorgement

A lot of women have an oversupply of milk when they first start to breastfeed their baby. This usually settles down by six weeks, but initially the engorgement can cause some attachment problems. Your baby will find it difficult to get on if the breast is really full and hard, or he might take himself off when the let-down comes if it is too fast for him to cope with.

If your breasts are really full, your nipples can flatten and your baby will find it hard to get a good mouthful of breast. The way to deal with this is to express a bit of milk so the breast is softened and the baby is able to get a good mouthful when attaching. You can either hand-express into a cup or a cloth but if you find this difficult then use a hand pump or electric pump to express a small amount until the breast has softened slightly.

If the let-down is coming too quickly and your baby pulls off, express until you get the let-down and then attach the baby. That way the flow will be more consistent when the baby goes on and he should be able to cope better.

Make sure your baby finishes one breast before you swap him to the other breast so he gets all the foremilk and the good fatty milk after that. If you swap breasts too soon, he can get a hit of foremilk from both breasts. Without any of the fat milk, he can get an overload of lactose, which can cause him to have a sore tummy and explosive, frothy poos.

## — Sore nipples

Sore nipples are a common problem when you first start to breastfeed. This discomfort can be relieved by ensuring your baby is attaching properly. Poor attachment is the main cause of cracked nipples. Some women do just have very sensitive nipples, however, and even when the baby is feeding in the correct position they can still experience very sore, even cracked nipples. You should, however, try to continue feeding when you have sore nipples and try not to miss feeds.

Ways to relieve sore nipples include applying warm cloths to your breasts or standing in a warm shower and letting the water run over them. You can rub expressed milk into your nipples, which will soften them and also promote healing. When feeding, offer the less sore breast first and try different feeding positions. Try to keep your nipples dry. Try not to wear tight bras or clothing and if you can, leave your breast exposed to the air as long as possible. This might be difficult if you have visitors but do the best you can.

If the soreness is getting worse or not getting better after a few days then I would recommend you get some help. A first line of help would be to contact the ABA. The ABA has a 24-hour helpline. Alternatively you can get private help from a lactation consultant or speak to the nurse at your local baby health clinic.

## — Mastitis

Mastitis is an infection of the breast tissue usually caused when bacteria enters the breast either through a crack or break in the skin or through the milk ducts. But you don't have to have sore nipples to get mastitis.

Symptoms of mastitis include:

+ breast tenderness
+ breast feels warm or hot to the touch
+ swelling of the breast
+ a general feeling of unwellness
+ flu-like symptoms, including aches, chills, fever and tiredness.

The usual treatment for mastitis is antibiotics, so if you suspect you have it then see your GP sooner rather than later. Sometimes symptoms can disappear or at least start to be relieved after 24 hours, so you may want to wait for a day before starting the antibiotics.

If you have mastitis, the best remedy is to keep feeding your baby. If feeding is just too painful, then express the milk and try to recommence feeding as soon as you can. Other things that can help include:

+ applying heat to the sore area and gently massaging the breast
+ taking pain relief (something that is okay for breastfeeding mothers) and getting some rest.

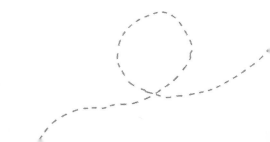

## — Blocked ducts

A blocked duct can cause a baby to fuss while feeding. This is because the flow of the milk will be affected by the blockage. You can usually feel a hard lump in your breast when you have a blocked duct but as long as you continue to feed the baby on that side the blockage should resolve within 24 to 48 hours. Point your baby's chin towards the blockage while feeding as the baby's sucking is the best way to get rid of it. You can also use heat and massage on the area.

### Expressing

Expressing can be a great way to continue breastfeeding your baby for a long time. If you express milk then you can have a longer period of time away from your baby than the usual two or three hours until she is due to be fed again. It can also mean that you can get a decent block of sleep overnight if your partner is able to give the baby a bottle of expressed breast milk (EBM).

I am a fan of expressing but I advise that you wait until your milk supply has been established and the baby has the attachment sorted. This means waiting about two to three weeks after the birth before you start to express.

There are two ways of expressing: either with your hands or with a pump. The pump is a more efficient and faster way of expressing but if you have a great supply then hand-expressing can be efficient as well. Breast pumps are either manual or electric and there is not much difference between them. The electric one can be faster and you can do both breasts at once if you need to.

The manual one is just as effective and can take a bit longer, but it is much more portable.

When you start expressing you need to make sure that all your equipment is sterile and you have washed your hands. Then sit yourself in a nice, quiet and relaxed position in the house. You can begin by using your hand to get to the let-down stage if you like, or if you go straight onto the pump then make sure the suction is gentle. Pumps can cause grazing and cracked nipples if the suction is too strong.

Some mothers like to look at a picture of their baby or think about them as this can help with the let-down. But whatever you do, make sure you are comfortable and that you have plenty of time to relax during the expressing.

### How to care for your precious breast milk

Research has shown that EBM:

+ can be stored at room temperature (less than 24°C) for eight hours
+ can be stored in the fridge for up to five days — store it in the back of the fridge where it is coldest
+ absorbs smells from the container or fridge, so use an odourless, sterilised container with a lid
+ can be stored in the freezer (a normal fridge freezer) for three months
+ once thawed should be used within four hours if it hasn't been warmed or it can be stored in the fridge for 24 hours

+ if it has been warmed then you can store it in the fridge *only* for four hours.

### Tips for storing your breast milk

+ When freezing breast milk, leave some space at the top of the container, as the milk expands as it freezes.
+ Freeze in small amounts to avoid unnecessary wastage — 50 ml is probably enough.
+ To defrost frozen milk, either put it in the fridge overnight or place it under warm running water (not hot). You can also put it out on the kitchen bench and let it defrost in its own time.
+ Fat in breast milk will separate and rise to the top so gently swirl the bottle to remix the milk. *Do not* shake the milk.

### How often should I feed my baby and how much does she need?

A newborn baby can feed anywhere from every two hours to every four hours. I don't encourage mothers to feed any more often than two hourly as doing so can cause more problems rather than alleviate them. The amount of time it takes to feed a baby can also vary but usually a newborn baby will take 40 to 60 minutes to get enough milk to last her for a couple of hours.

A bottle-fed baby usually doesn't take as long to finish a feed, but it is important to make sure she is not gulping the milk or drinking too quickly as this can give her tummy pain or lots of unnecessary wind. Make sure you are using a newborn teat and if she does gulp that you stop the feed every 20 millilitres, sit her up and allow her to burp before continuing with the feed.

There are some babies who sleep and sleep and sleep when they are tiny. It is important that the baby doesn't sleep too much though, and then miss feeds. A newborn baby needs a minimum of six feeds every 24 hours, so if your baby is sleeping too much you will need to wake her to ensure she is fed every four hours. Some babies who have had some jaundice can be more sleepy than others, so it is important to monitor how many feeds she is having and make sure she gets a good one when she does feed.

My policy when breastfeeding newborns, to ensure your baby is getting enough milk, is that she should be having 20 minutes of continual sucking. It can take up to an hour for her to have the full 20 minutes as she might be a baby who stops and starts, as a lot of newborns do. But it is really important that if she is falling asleep during the feed and she hasn't had those 20 minutes of active sucking, that you wake her up and persevere with the feed.

It can be difficult sometimes to keep a newborn baby awake, or wake her up once she has fallen asleep. If you are struggling with this just let her have a five-minute nap then try to continue with the feed. A good way to try to get a baby to wake up is to leave the nappy change until the middle of the feed or until she starts to fall asleep. This can often help her to wake up with all the action going on in the nappy area. You can also sit her up and burp her before or after the nappy change to get her wide awake and ready to continue with the feed.

The reason the feed shouldn't take longer than 60 minutes is because after being awake for an hour and feeding during that time, a baby will be tired and ready for sleep again. So because you don't want to miss that sleep window and have an overtired baby, an hour of feeding is the limit.

If you are bottle-feeding and the feed takes less than one hour, then you can have the rest of the hour to connect with and chat to your new baby.

## Bottle-feeding

If you are bottle-feeding your baby then you need to choose a formula. There are countless formulas on the market and sometimes it is a matter of just choosing one and giving it a go. If you find your baby is not very happy on that particular formula then you could try another one, but give it a good go before you change. This is unless she has a reaction to the formula. If she vomits large amounts of formula back, has increasing tummy pain or explosive poos, that would most likely mean that particular formula is not for her.

### *Safe bottle-feeding*

Always make sure you test the temperature of the milk before you give it to your baby. The best way to test it is to pour a little bit out onto the inside of your wrist. The milk should be warm but not hot.

To heat the formula you can use a bottle warmer, which will heat the milk slowly. A lot of people opt to heat bottles in the microwave. You need to be aware that the milk can continue to heat after you have taken the bottle out of the microwave, so always shake the bottle well and check the milk is not too hot.

## Burping, vomiting and pooing

Okay, now we will get down to the basics! A newborn baby is all about bodily functions, and you will find that you become increasingly focused on and perhaps a bit obsessed with what comes out of your baby's body.

Because a baby's digestive system is immature she needs help to get up all the wind she swallows when she feeds. Usually breastfed babies are not as burpy as bottle-fed babies but there is always an exception to that, and I have heard some of the biggest burps come out of the tiniest, breastfed babies.

You need to burp the baby when she starts to fuss on the breast or bottle, and this can be after five, ten or 20 minutes of feeding. If a baby is fussing the first thing to think of is wind. Sit her up on your lap, or put her up over your shoulder and wait till she burps. There is no need to pat your baby on the back to get the burp up — all she really needs is to be in an upright position — but a gentle rub on the back can be comforting and soothing for her.

You need to burp her again once the feed has finished, even if she is asleep. Just gently sit her upright and wait for the burp to come up. If after about five minutes of being upright nothing has come up, assume there might not be one this time. But do give your baby every opportunity to get that wind up, so if you are sitting her up and she is squirming then assume a burp is on its way. After the feed, keep your baby upright until all the squirming has stopped, then you can get on with the settling.

Young babies can also be a bit vomity. These little vomits of undigested milk are called possits. They are completely normal as long as your baby is not distressed by the possiting. If she does scream or cry after possiting then she might have some reflux, so it could be worth discussing that with your GP or paediatrician. Projectile vomiting is not normal either, so if your baby has large projectile vomits get her checked out by your GP or paediatrician.

Pooing is another bodily function you will be focused on once you have a baby. A new baby's poo is usually a mustard colour and a pasty consistency. You may occasionally find what look like mustard seeds in it — this is normal. A breastfed baby can poo anywhere from once or twice every time she feeds to once a week, so don't panic if your baby only poos weekly. It is very uncommon for a breastfed baby to be constipated, so as long as when she does go it is that pasty consistency then everything is normal.

Bottle-fed babies can get constipated, especially if you are changing formulas. Constipated poo is small, hard little pebbles and you may see her straining and going very red in the face when she is trying to go. She may also cry. This could indicate that she is constipated. A bottle-fed baby should poo about once a day. Keep an eye on those poos, and, if they are soft and pasty, everything is fine.

## Reflux

Putting it simply, reflux is the regurgitation of milk and acids found in the stomach. This regurgitation causes the baby pain and can mean you have a very unsettled and unhappy little baby.

Reflux can be over-diagnosed and a lot of unsettled babies are automatically assumed to have reflux when really they are just overtired and need some sleep. So first make sure that your baby does not have a sleep problem.

Generally all babies have some regurgitation and for most babies it doesn't cause them any discomfort or distress. If your baby is very unsettled, however, crying a lot during and after the feed, vomity and perhaps not gaining much weight then she could have reflux.

Some babies who have reflux don't show any major symptoms although they might have sleeping issues like catnapping during the day or waking frequently at night. They may like to comfort suck or only snack on their feed — take a small feed and then stop. These can also be symptoms of reflux.

## CASE STUDY
### Molly

Molly's parents were baffled as there was no way they could get her to sleep for more than 30 to 40 minutes at a time during the day. The nights weren't so bad but she did wake frequently and was fed pretty much every three hours overnight. They also told me she was a pretty happy baby when she was awake and was gaining good amounts of weight.

I thought it was a classic case of a catnapping six week old, so I gave them a program to follow and talked them through the

Babybliss Settling Technique and how they were to get Molly to go back to sleep once she had woken. They tried diligently for a couple of weeks to get her to sleep longer but she couldn't get past that 30 minutes of sleep during the day. I decided to visit them to see what was going on.

It didn't take me long to work out that Molly had reflux. She was doing lots and lots of gulping hours after her last feed and I could hear her swallowing the milk back down after it was coming up into her throat. She also fed for a shorter period of time than a baby of her age should. She was a happy baby but at that 30-minute mark, when she woke from her nap, she cried and cried and only picking her up consoled her.

It is nearly impossible to teach a baby with reflux to sleep if the reflux is not being treated. As well as booking her an appointment with her GP, I showed her parents how to deal with reflux at home. These tips included keeping her upright for 20 minutes after the feed and elevating the head of the cot. I explained that they needed to keep trying to get her back to sleep when she woke and once her medication was working the settling technique should be more effective and she should start to sleep better.

It took about two weeks to get Molly to sleep better both day and night.

# Development and stimulation

Lots of things are happening in the first six weeks of your baby's life. Babies develop at different rates and you may have a baby who is content to remain sleepy and peaceful for a few more weeks after he is born or you may have a baby who comes into the world with his eyes wide open and raring to get on with life. All babies are different so try not to compare your baby to the other babies in your mothers' group. As long as your baby is active, eating, sleeping and gaining weight then you have nothing to be worried about.

A newborn baby doesn't know he is a separate person from you. He doesn't know who is going to care for him, feed him or who will come to him when he cries. A newborn baby will cry when he is hungry and tired, and he needs you to respond to his cry.

When your baby is born he won't be able to support his head and his little hands will grasp around things, like your finger. He will also startle at loud noises and could make funny animal-like sounds when sleeping and sometimes when feeding. A newborn baby can hear. He will find it difficult to focus on objects but can see things up close.

A newborn has no control over his movements; it is all reflexes and involuntary reactions. After about a month, however, he should be able to lift his head briefly when he is lying on his tummy and might start to kick his legs at about six weeks. Any time after four weeks your baby will start to smile spontaneously at you. He learns to do this by looking at your face and he starts to take an interest in that soon after he is born. It is really important that he can see your face and see it smile and that you talk to him in a soothing voice. This is how he will get to know you and will start to recognise you.

## Playing with your baby

A newborn baby doesn't have much time for play. His awake-time is pretty much taken up with feeding, nappy changing, burping and settling, leaving minimal time for much else. A newborn also gets overtired very quickly with all the new stimulation, so it is important to keep the activity and interaction gentle and soothing.

Activities you can do with your new baby include stroking or massaging his little body, speaking or singing to him softly, playing music to him, cuddling him and holding him in your arms and rocking him.

*This Babybliss newborn log (opposite)*
*is useful for keeping track of*
*your baby's day*

(There are also several more copies
of this log on pages 269–275)

## Babybliss Newborn Log

| Time feed started | How long on left breast? | How long on right breast? | Bowels (tick) | Wet nappy (tick) | Awake from when to when? | Total awake time | Slept for how long? (From when to when?) | Total time asleep |
|---|---|---|---|---|---|---|---|---|
| | | | | | | | | |
| | | | | | | | | |
| | | | | | | | | |
| | | | | | | | | |
| | | | | | | | | |
| | | | | | | | | |
| | | | | | | | | |
| | | | | | | | | |
| | | | | | | | | |
| | | | | | | | | |
| | | | | | | | | |
| | | | | | | | | |
| | | | | | | | | |

# Chapter 5

# Working towards a contented baby: six to 12 weeks

# Baby sleeping

Between six and 12 weeks of age you can start to get a routine happening or at least notice patterns in your baby's awake time and with her sleeping. It is around six weeks when babies become aware of the difference between day and night, and they may sleep longer at night and be more wakeful during the day. It is because of this development that babies start to catnap during the day — that is, they sleep for only one sleep cycle, which can be from 30 to 45 minutes. Now is the time to work on getting your baby to be a great sleeper.

## When should my baby sleep and for how long?

Around six weeks your baby should still be sleeping between her feeds and should really only be awake for 60 minutes at a time. This can occasionally extend to 70 or 80 minutes, but you would not want her to be up for more than 90 minutes.

By 12 weeks you would want your baby to have three definite day sleeps and be sleeping for 90 to 120 minutes for the first two sleeps of the day with the late afternoon sleep being anywhere from 45 to 90 minutes.

| Age | Up-time | Down-time | Average sleeps |
|---|---|---|---|
| 6 weeks | Approx 1 hour, but no longer than 1½ hours | Ranging from 2 to 3 hours | Four to five sleeps in 24 hours |
| 12 weeks | Around 1½ hours | 1½ to 2½ hours | Three definite day sleeps, two long and one shorter |

## Realistic expectations about your baby's sleeping routine

While it is great to have a baby who is sleeping well at night, it is also important not to put too much pressure on yourself or your baby to get him to sleep longer if he is not ready for it. Young babies need to be fed regularly and so it is unrealistic to expect a baby of this age to go longer than about five or six hours without a feed — and that is fantastic if he does sleep for that long. I often get calls and emails from mothers asking why their eight-week-old baby isn't sleeping through the night because all the babies at their mothers' group are or their friend's baby slept through from six weeks. By 12 weeks, if your baby is sleeping five or six hours overnight, this is considered sleeping all night. So take the pressure off yourself and your little one. Smile politely and congratulate those mothers who tell you they have an exceptional baby, and work on getting a routine established because that is often what prompts a baby to sleep longer.

## Babybliss routine and ritual

*Getting your baby to sleep longer in the daytime*

After about six weeks you can start to work on having a more definite structure to your day. Your baby can now naturally fall into having three to four daytime sleeps and then may start to sleep for longer periods overnight. But if during this time he is not doing it naturally, it is important for you to know that you can start to teach him.

So begin the day with a definite starting time. Between 6.30 and 7 am is a good time for a small baby to start the day, but this could extend to 7.30 or 8 am if that better suits you and the baby. This way you can have the baby up for a certain amount of time — at this age for up to 90 minutes — and then he is down for a certain amount of time, until he is due to feed again. This means that you can fit three to four sleeps in during the daylight hours, working towards having three definite sleeps during the day by 12 weeks of age.

A good example of a routine for this age would be:

| | |
|---|---|
| 6.30 or 7 am | First daytime wake-up. Get up. Small activity like nappy change or some chit-chat with Mum and/or Dad (five to 10 minutes is enough). Feed — a nappy change in the middle of the feed if you need to wake him up or he needs one. More quiet activity — burp baby, some play on the floor or in a rocker. Wind-down time — wrap baby up, comforting pat, soothing words or a soft song. |
| 7.30 or 8 am | Back to bed |

Your baby should not be up for more than 90 minutes at a time, but may only last 60 minutes or so. Watch your baby for any tired signs he may display. At the first tired sign, usually a yawn, wrap your baby and start preparing to wind him down. If you haven't got to this stage by the time your baby yawns twice then you really need to get a move on.

At this age tired signs can be:

✦ grizzling or crying

✦ increasingly jerky movements of his arms and legs

✦ staring into space

✦ clenching his fists

✦ grimacing

✦ yawning

✦ any combination of the above.

The routine needs to continue on like this for the rest of the day. You watch for tired signs but also be aware that if he has been up for 90 minutes or close to it, he needs to go to bed, whether he is displaying tired signs or not. This is a really important point and relates back to watching and getting to know your baby. Some babies display very clear tired signs and some don't display any. In fact, some babies can wind up when they are tired, tricking you into thinking they are really alert and awake and not ready for sleep. Don't be fooled! Your baby needs to go to sleep and will only continue to get more tired if you don't get him down and off to sleep.

### Catnapping

Around this age your baby might start to catnap a little more. By that I mean he will sleep for only about 30 to 45 minutes, then wake looking like he has just had the best sleep possible. Most babies go through this catnapping phase and, left to their own devices would continue to sleep only in short bursts, for that one sleep cycle, if you let them. My way of teaching a baby to get past this catnapping phase is to have him in the cot for as long as he is supposed to be asleep. And at this age it would be when he is next due a feed. In a way you are telling his little body clock that he is actually supposed to stay asleep for longer than one sleep cycle.

A lot of parents, when this phase happens, fall into the trap of getting their baby up when he wakes at the end of his first sleep cycle because he looks like he is wide awake. But what will happen is after you get him up he won't last for the 90 minutes he is supposed to be up for and will start displaying tired signs after 30 minutes or so. So he will get put back down again sooner than you would have done normally. This can go on all day and any kind of routine or structure goes out the window. The baby will never learn to sleep longer if this is what you do, and there is no rhythm to the day as the baby is constantly up and down and everyone gets confused, overtired and frantic. Every day will be a bit different too because your baby might fall asleep with tiredness and sleep for two hours and then the next day you are back to 30-minute sleeps. It is really important to have structure and teach your baby to sleep for more than one sleep cycle.

That is all well and good, I hear you say, but how do I do that? Good question!

The best way to teach a baby to sleep longer in his daytime naps is to resettle him to sleep until he is due for his next feed. Resettling can be challenging, especially when you first start to do it, so when your baby wakes wait to see what he does. If he is happy and not crying, leave him in his cot — don't go to him. Once he starts to complain, go to him and make sure he is still wrapped up nice and tightly. If not, rewrap him as quickly as you can. Then put him back into his cot, on his back, and pat him gently on his chest, up near his shoulder or arm. The pat should be a nice rhythmical pat at the pace of a heartbeat, and while you pat you should also be shooshing him. You need to continue this patting until the baby goes back to sleep.

If your baby gets really distressed while you are resettling him, then pick him up and calm and settle him by patting in your arms.

If you do pick the baby up, don't walk him around the house — keep him in his room, close to the cot. This is sleep time, and he needs to know that.

Always try to get him back into the cot before he is sound asleep and do the last bit of the settling in the cot, but don't stress if you can't do this and you have to hold him in your arms until he is asleep. The main objective is to get the baby back to sleep, so if you have to do that in your arms then so be it. Once he is asleep though, he needs to go back into his bed for the remainder of the sleep. But try to work towards doing all the resettling in his cot once your baby has become used to the resettling technique.

When resettling your baby, it can be a good idea to use a dummy. If you haven't used one to date, then it would be reasonable to introduce it if your baby is under 12 weeks. When first using the dummy, you may need to hold it in your baby's mouth for a minute or two until they get the hang of sucking it, and once they are sucking the dummy it should work to help calm the baby down. So when resettling, pop the dummy in and use the patting technique to get your baby back to sleep. You might have to put the dummy in a few times but once your baby is calm and goes off to sleep, he will spit the dummy out. Don't try to put the dummy in if he doesn't want it or is asleep.

Your baby will definitely go back to sleep if he is not due for a feed and it is up to you to teach him how to do this by being consistent in the way you deal with the wakes. Therefore, every time you resettle him you must do it the same way. This means that after only a short period of time your baby will remember what you are doing, the process will become familiar to him and he will resist less and less. Don't give up in the middle of resettling. It may take 30 to 45 minutes to get a baby to go back to sleep, as he may not feel tired again for about that long. Persevere until it is done so the next time it will be easier. Eventually what happens is the baby will start to put himself back to sleep after that first sleep cycle or he will sleep on past that first sleep cycle, which means you won't have to bother with any more resettles.

## CASE STUDY
### Olie

Olie was a classic catnapper and when his mother contacted me she was really at her wits' end as nothing she did could get him to sleep more than 40 to 45 minutes at a time during the day. When I saw him he was such a tired little baby and by the end of the day he was so upset and unsettled, he would take hours and hours to finally get off to sleep.

It can take time to teach a baby to sleep longer than one sleep cycle and it is really important that you are consistent when you start to teach them. Babies need consistency and repetition so they can become familiar with the process or technique you are using and become less resistant and easier to settle.

I explained to Olie's mum how important it was to *not* get him up when he woke after that one sleep cycle. The way to teach a baby to sleep longer is to keep him in his cot for as long as he is supposed to be asleep and if he wakes before he is due to get up then you need to resettle him until he goes back to sleep.

At Olie's age there was no way he shouldn't be able to go back to sleep because he was so young and really needed to have more sleep. So while I was with them I demonstrated how Olie's mum needed to pat him back to sleep when he woke.

The first time we resettled him it took quite a while to get him back to sleep but then he slept for another 90 minutes. I find this can often be the case. Once you get a baby back to sleep after that first sleep cycle then he can sleep for two sleep cycles before waking again.

Olie's mum then used the technique for the rest of the day and managed to get another good sleep out of him after a bit of resettling. Then after another day she reported that the resettling was taking a lot less time and he had on a few occasions slept through that first sleep cycle on his own.

It took about seven days to get Olie over his catnapping and this was because his mum was absolutely consistent in her approach to getting him back to sleep. She did the same thing every time he woke and he eventually began to understand. With the extra sleep he was less overtired, easier to settle and able to sleep for longer.

## Establishing a bedtime

As well as having a definite start to the day and nap times, your baby also needs to have a definite bedtime. This means that your baby goes to bed 'for the night' at the same time every evening. This should be between 6 and 7 pm every night, which means he remains in his bed overnight, except when he is being fed, until it is time to get up in the morning and start the day. A lot of parents get their baby up again around 8.30 to 9 pm when he wakes, play with him, and treat it as another awake period for the baby. But I believe that it is important to establish a bedtime ritual as soon as you can with your baby. Bedtime should be bedtime and there is no playtime after that. The baby gets up to feed, has a nappy change and then is settled back to bed until he is due to be fed again.

When you are establishing the definite bedtime you can also begin to build a ritual around going to bed. The ritual you begin will be continued throughout your child's young life. Children respond to ritual and develop expectations from a very young age, so a ritual around sleep will help your child. Wrapping your baby is part of the sleep ritual as you always wrap your baby before you put him to bed. An example of a bedtime ritual for a baby this age could be:

✦ wrap your baby
✦ close the curtains while holding him
✦ cradle him in your arms and sing a lullaby
✦ kiss him and tell him it is 'sleepy time'
✦ put him into his cot, give him a couple of pats and then leave the room.

The evenings can be a bit tricky and are often referred to as the 'witching hours' because babies can often be unsettled and difficult to get to sleep for a variety of reasons. One of these is that at the end of the day we are all tired, a baby even more so as she is taking on so much stimulation when she is awake. I also think that if you are breastfeeding your milk supply can drop off a bit at this time of the day causing your baby to be a bit hungrier than she has been earlier.

One good way of dealing with this difficult time is to just feed your baby more frequently than you would normally. If it has been two hours or close to it since the last feed, I recommend feeding her again and hopefully that will help her to settle. You can also bath your baby at this time of the night to help calm her and get her into a sleepy mood. Try doing half the feed, then into a nice warm bath, then finish the feed, wrap her up nice and tightly and get her to sleep.

If your baby is overtired then you might need to hold her until she goes off to sleep, which is absolutely fine at this time of the day. Again, if it has been at least two hours since the last feed then feed her. This is known as 'cluster feeding' and will not only help your baby go off to sleep when she is unsettled at the end of the day, but may also help her to sleep longer overnight as she has a really full tummy. A lovely warm and relaxing bath can help her drift off to sleep and stay there for at least three to four hours.

## Sleeping summary

This is the stage in your baby's development to get her really sleeping well between her feeds both during the day and night but it can also be the age when your baby starts to catnap during the day. You can get longer stretches out of her overnight and you can work on getting her sleeping longer than one sleep cycle during the day, by resettling her every time she wakes before she is due to be fed.

Use a dummy if you need to, to help with resettling and you can introduce cluster feeding in the evenings to help deal with this more difficult part of the day.

Remember, you are working towards having a baby who will self-settle, so try to minimise your intervention when getting your baby to sleep initially and don't be afraid to put her down to sleep when she is awake.

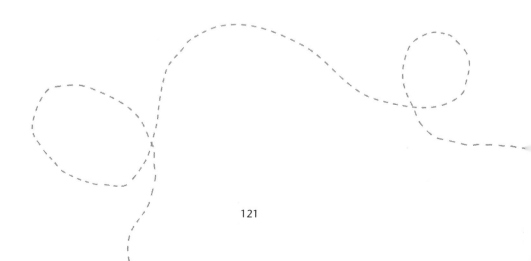

# Baby feeding

Now you can start to have more of a pattern in the way your baby is feeding because at this age most babies will naturally begin to fall into a three-hour or four-hour feeding pattern. If you are still feeding a bit more often, then you can commence to stretch the feeds out to at least three hours between them or pretty close to that during the day.

If you are breastfeeding your baby, you will notice that at around six weeks your breast milk will settle down. Your milk supply becomes much more a supply–demand system rather than your breasts just filling up after every feed, so you may notice that you are not so big and full all the time.

It is around this time too that the length of the feeds will become shorter. This is because your baby will have mastered the attachment by now and so will you. She is also much more awake and focused on the feeding, rather than dropping off to sleep. So instead of taking the full hour, you may have the feed down to 30 or 40 minutes.

Babies of this age are also able to cope with a little more activity than when they were newborns. She will be more alert, so she can spend time on a mat on the floor or have more time with you chit-chatting away. This is also a good time to start not feeding her as soon as she opens her eyes. Get her up and have a little bit of interaction with her before feeding her. This way she will start not to expect a feed every time she opens her eyes and that association will diminish.

## How often should I feed my baby and how much does she need?

By now you should have a pretty good routine established with the feeding and know when your baby needs to be fed. At this age most babies will remain on the three- to four-hourly feeding schedule and no longer need those two-hour feeds, except maybe in the evenings if they are having a melt-down or a growth spurt.

Some babies will begin to sleep longer at night and you may be feeding only twice overnight, which is a great thing to aim for if it isn't already happening.

If you are breastfeeding then your baby will most probably be taking one breast completely and then some of the second one. If you aren't already offering the second breast because you have had sufficient milk offering just one, and your baby is becoming a bit unsettled and difficult to put to sleep or stay asleep then it might be worth starting to offer that second breast.

If you are bottle-feeding your baby then feed her according to what is indicated on the product. If your baby is regularly finishing the bottle and looking like she could take some more, then offer her some more milk. Some big babies need more milk and so it is worthwhile filling them up so they will continue to grow well, which also means they will sleep well until they are due to be fed again.

## Dropping feeds at night

Dropping feeds can happen in two ways: your baby will naturally start to sleep longer overnight and sleep through a feed, or you teach her to sleep longer. You may notice that she might start lasting four, five or even six hours before she wakes for a feed. And often this may happen for two sleep periods in a row, but one session of long sleep is great too. The most common development is that she will start to have a long sleep in the evening. For example, after you put her down for the night at 6 or 7 pm she might have a five-hour sleep and then wake around midnight for a feed. Then she might go back to wanting to be fed every three to four hours, which is fine.

This longer sleep period might also occur after midnight if you have cluster fed your baby before putting her down to sleep at night. This too is okay and, in fact, the regular feeding might contribute to her then sleeping for a longer period overnight.

I recommend working towards the one longer period of sleep overnight, be that before or after midnight. Ideally, you would want to be feeding around 10 pm, then around 3 am and then maybe 6 am. Obviously this timing is flexible as it depends on your baby, but those times between feeds are a good example of what you would want to work towards.

Bigger babies can sleep better overnight and be the first to drop feeds. This is because they are usually big feeders, taking in lots of kilojoules and can therefore last a bit longer between feeds. But then there are some tiny babies who just do it naturally.

I recommend that at this age babies still be fed overnight — absolutely. But you can start to experiment a bit to see if she can last a little longer, especially by 12 weeks of age. If, for example, you have fed your baby at 10 or 11 pm and then she wakes again at 1 am, try to resettle her to see if she will go back to sleep without being fed. You can do this by using a dummy, which can be a great way to get a baby back to sleep with minimal fuss, or you can use the settling technique of patting and shooshing her back to sleep. But don't leave her to cry on her own. A baby of this age needs to be helped back to sleep, just as you help her to sleep longer during the day. Little babies need to be taught how to sleep longer in a gentle manner.

If you have been trying to get your baby back to sleep for 30 to 45 minutes and she is still wide awake then she probably does need to be fed, so get her up and feed her. If she wakes again the next night, do the same, so you are essentially stretching her by about 30 minutes. You may then find that she just naturally starts to sleep to this later time. After a week or more of her waking at this new time, you can then try to stretch her again by 30 minutes or so. This method will get her used to sleeping longer between feeds.

## More 'you' time

When your baby reaches this age you can start to feel like you are coming out of the fog of having a newborn and be ready and able to have some more time for yourself. This is because your baby will be heading towards a more structured day, with definite times for sleep and activity. So you can plan your day with a little more confidence.

You have probably been feeling at times that since you had your baby you just can't get a moment to do the basic things, and this is an absolutely normal feeling when you have a new baby. I had a friend who called me one day in despair saying she couldn't believe she had turned into one of 'those women' who was still in her pyjamas at three o'clock in the afternoon. I told her to take a deep breath and relax. Who was going to see her anyway, and her baby didn't care how she was dressed!

I do know that it can be stressful when you feel things are falling apart around you and all you seem to be doing is feeding your baby and then trying to get her to sleep. That is why it is beneficial to be working towards a routine for both you and your baby. That way both of you have a rhythm to your day and know pretty much what will happen from one activity to the next. It is encouraging for you to be able to plan activities that you have been putting on the back burner over the last six weeks, like catching up with friends, or venturing out to the shopping centre to have a look at the world outside — and do a bit of shopping, of course.

That said, don't put pressure on yourself to get out and about if that is not what you feel like doing. Just like in the first six weeks of your baby's life, time at home is really important, for you both. Babies love being at home, as do all children — it is their sanctuary and where they feel most secure. Children pester their parents when they are out with the question 'Can we go home now?' So there's no reason to feel bad about your baby spending a lot of time at home. It is more for your sake that you need to get out, just so you don't go stir crazy.

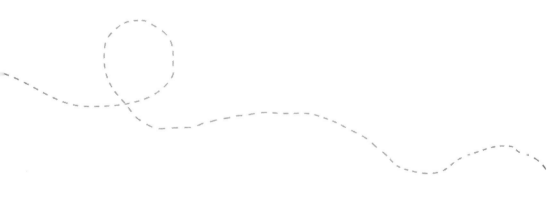

# Development and stimulation

Between about six and eight weeks of age you will notice that your baby will be watching your face when you talk to him and will almost look like he is listening to what you say. He might even start to mimic you by moving his mouth. He may also be starting to make different noises other than crying and begin to sound like he is trying to talk to you.

Your baby should be smiling at you by now and by 12 weeks can be laughing out loud. You may also notice that when you put your baby down on his tummy for 'tummy time' he will start to lift his head up off the mat. Also, when your baby is on his back he will start to kick his legs out strongly, looking like he is really enjoying his time on the mat. When playing with him, he will start to follow an object moved in an arc above his face.

I have mentioned the 'witching hour', which is when a baby just seems to be really unsettled no matter what you do. This hour (or two, or three) usually happens in the afternoon or evening and is associated with a lot more crying than your baby has done in the rest of the day. It is common for a baby of this age to start to cry a bit more than he has previously and a lot of people try to explain it by saying the baby has 'colic' or some other thing that is causing him to cry. Now while in some cases this may be the case, I think that mostly the behaviour is just because it is the end of the day and the baby is overwhelmed by all that is going on around him and inside him. We all get tired at the end of the day and your baby is no exception — in fact babies get more tired than all of us. They are constantly being exposed to new stimulation and have no idea what is going on from one moment to the next.

Try to be patient when your baby is in this 'witching hour'. If it means feeding him a bit more frequently or giving him a nice warm bath to help calm, that's fine. Remember to try to remain calm and quiet yourself and, rest assured, this time will pass.

## Developmental milestones

During six to 12 weeks your baby should:

+ smile in response to you
+ follow an object moved above his face
+ lift his head when lying on his tummy
+ kick both his legs
+ watch your face intently and appear to listen to your voice
+ start to make sounds other than crying and respond to sounds
+ laugh out loud by three months.

## Playing with your baby

When your baby is about six weeks old you will notice he is becoming much more alert and taking in his surroundings. He will also be able to stay awake for a bit longer so you will have more time when he is not feeding or sleeping.

At this young age babies don't really play with toys but they can lie under a baby gym or sit in a rocker, or have some quality time sitting and 'chatting' to you. Other things you can do to stimulate your baby are:

+ baby massage
+ hang a mobile above him and watch him be fascinated by the movement
+ speak to him in a gentle and calm manner so he can see your face
+ sing to him or play him music
+ rock him in your arms or a rocker.

Chapter 6

# The interactive baby: 12 to 18 weeks

# Baby sleeping

By now you will have noticed that your baby is a real little person, with her own personality and temperament. This is a lovely age too, because you as parents are now off your training wheels and should be feeling confident and assured, except of course for the odd little hiccup here and there.

It is around this age that I recommend you really start to have a more structured routine in the day and night. For the last 12 weeks you have been dealing with so much new information and trying to work out how this little person ticks that it can all become a bit of a blur and you may not be really sure what is happening from one day to the next. Now it is time for you to have more control of the situation. When your day is structured you can plan outings and activities and not just play everything by ear.

Babies love routine and you will too — I can guarantee it!

## When should my baby sleep and for how long?

At about 12 weeks your baby will move from having usually four sleeps during the day to having three sleeps during the day, ranging from about one-and-a-half to two-and-a-half hours at a time, or a total of about four-and-a-half to six hours per day. She should also now be moving towards getting about 11 to 12 hours sleep overnight, with a late evening feed and an early morning feed thrown in.

Between 12 and 18 weeks you should notice that your baby will be able to stay awake for longer periods during the day. By 18 weeks she could even manage being up for close to two hours at a time. This usually happens in the middle of the day, rather than the beginning or the end. Babies usually get tired more quickly in the mornings and so, after they have risen for the day, had a feed and a play, they often start to display tired signs early. Make sure she has been up for at least close to 90 minutes but don't push it any longer if she looks like she needs to go back to sleep.

At this age tired signs can be the same as when she was younger, and include:

- ✦ grizzling or crying
- ✦ increasing jerky movements of the arms and legs
- ✦ staring into space
- ✦ clenching of the fists
- ✦ grimacing
- ✦ yawning
- ✦ rubbing the eyes or face
- ✦ pulling at the ears
- ✦ or any combination of the above.

Remember to watch for the tired signs but also keep an eye on the clock. You don't want your baby to get overtired because then she will have difficulty getting to sleep and often sleep worse than she should. And as I mentioned elsewhere, some babies don't display tired signs, which is why you need to watch the clock.

So in summary:

| Age | Up-time | Down-time | Average sleeps |
|---|---|---|---|
| 12 weeks | Around 1½ hours | 1½ to 2½ hours | Three definite day sleeps: two long and one shorter. |
| 18 weeks | 1½ to 2 hours (2 hours only once per day) | 1½ to 2½ hours | Three definite day sleeps: two long and one shorter, and 11 to 12 hours overnight, with one to two feeds. |

## Babybliss routine and ritual

At this age you can really start to have a good routine and any ritual you have been doing around sleep time will become much more cemented in your baby's day. If you haven't started using a ritual around sleep times then I recommend you start now. Babies from a very young age can develop expectation, so start making things familiar to your child, especially the process of going to bed. If the ritual is repeated the same way every time the baby is put to bed, eventually she will become familiar with it and come to know what is going to happen. The ritual takes the surprise out of what is happening and means that she is less resistant to going down as she is aware that going to bed is the last step in this process.

A good ritual to use before bed is to wrap your baby, which is what most parents would still be doing at this age. Along with using the wrap you can close the blinds, give her a little cuddle and then turn the light off and put her into her bed. Some people use music in the bedtime ritual and that is absolutely fine. It doesn't really matter what you include in the ritual as long as it happens the same way every time your baby goes to bed.

A good routine for a baby of this age would be as follows:

| | |
|---|---|
| 4.30 to 5.30 am | Breastfeed or bottle-feed then straight back to sleep. (Note: if your baby sleeps through to 6 am it is okay to start the day then.) |
| 6.30 to 7 am | Up for the day. Babies should have some activity, then a feed, then some more activity and then be put back to bed. This cycle should last no longer than about 1½ hours. |

| | |
|---|---|
| Around 8 to 8.30 am | Morning sleep — this sleep should last about 2 hours but can be between 1½ and 3 hours. |
| 9.30 to 10 am | Up from sleep. Repeat the same activity/feed/activity cycle. This cycle can last up to 2 hours for this age. |
| 11.30 to 12 pm | Put baby down for the midday sleep. This sleep should last about 2 hours but can be between 1½ and 3 hours. |
| Around 1.30 to 2 pm | Up from sleep. Repeat the same activity/feed/activity cycle. This cycle can last from 1½ to 2 hours. |
| Around 3.30 | Put baby down for the afternoon sleep. This nap is traditionally a shorter nap and may only last for 30 to 45 minutes as your baby gets older. This is okay as this nap will be dropped at around six months. |
| 4.30 to 5 pm | Up from sleep. Do not let your baby sleep past 5 pm as you want her to go to bed for the night at around 6.30 to 7 pm at the latest and she won't be tired enough if she sleeps too late in the afternoon. |

| | |
|---|---|
| 6 to 7 pm | Bedtime ritual. This can include a bath, more quiet activity like a story, then a feed and then into bed. This ritual needs to be the same every night. |

### *Getting your baby to sleep longer at night*

Between 12 and 18 weeks you can really get your baby and yourself into a solid routine, especially at night. It is around this time that your baby should definitely be starting to sleep for longer periods overnight. If she hasn't begun to do this by herself then there are things you can do to get it happening. At this age your baby still needs to be fed overnight if she hasn't naturally started to sleep through, but you can establish a routine where she is getting her longest period of sleep over the middle of the night — and you can get some good rest too.

By now you should have a good night-time ritual established and your baby should also have a definite bedtime, which can be any time between 6 and 7 pm. Once your baby has gone down for the night she needs to stay there for the whole of the night, only getting up to feed and then going straight back to bed: no playtime, no chit-chat.

You will also notice now that your baby doesn't need to be awake for too long overnight. She will start to feed much more quickly and can go back to sleep without too much fuss. It is still important that you give her time to burp after you feed her but you may find that she is less bothered by wind and tummy pains than during the day.

The 'dream feed' is talked about a lot in parenting books and I do think it can be a great way to get babies sleeping till early morning. The dream feed is when you get your baby up out of bed — she is still asleep — and you feed her. You don't unwrap her, you don't change her nappy if it doesn't really need changing, and once you have fed her you put her back to bed quickly with little fuss. Essentially, the feed is being done in her sleep, or while she is very drowsy.

I encourage people to dream feed if they have a baby who is waking around 1 or 2 am. It is worth knowing that sometimes the dream feed doesn't work, however, and your baby may still wake at the time she was previously. If you want the technique to work, you need to give it a good go and you will need to resettle your baby, using the settling technique I have mentioned. Then ideally what should happen is that she will start to naturally sleep longer till around 4 or 5 am, when you can feed her and get her back to bed till 6.30 or 7 am.

Now obviously your decision on whether to do the dream feed depends on how you feel about a couple of things: do you want to stay up till 10.30 or 11 pm to give the dream feed, or is your baby naturally waking at this time anyway? If you are happy to go to bed early and then get up at 1 or 2 am to feed her and then she sleeps through to 6 or 7 am, then stick with that. Or if your baby is waking at some stage before midnight then you will just feed her anyway, and that is good too. But I encourage you to give the dream feed a go if you and your baby are not getting a big chunk of sleep overnight.

Dream feeding, however, may not be the miracle cure, and if your baby still wakes before 4 am then try to get her back to sleep without feeding, by using the resettling technique. After a couple of nights of doing this your baby should sleep to the early hours of the morning, when you will feed her and put her back to sleep till it is time to start the day.

### Catnapping

If your baby is only catnapping through the day then you need to look at the section on catnapping in the previous chapter (see page 114) and implement the Babybliss Settling Technique to get him to sleep for longer periods during the day.

If you deprive a baby of sleep during the day then he will not necessarily sleep better at night. I find the opposite is true and it becomes more obvious the older a baby is. So it is worthwhile really trying to get past the catnapping while he is still fairly young. If a baby doesn't get enough sleep during the day then he will be very difficult to get down for the night can wake more frequently than he needs to. This is because he is so overtired that he cannot get into his deep sleep. A baby who gets plenty of sleep during the day has a calmer and more relaxed way of going off to sleep and is able to get into deep sleep quickly without startling. I don't know about you but if I am very tired I often lie awake for ages running a million things around in my head. Your baby is the same and will find it difficult to relax enough to go into a deeper sleep. So sleep begets sleep — a great motto to remember!

### The dummy

Around this age you may find the dummy is still a useful aid in getting your baby to settle and go to sleep. If it is still useful then I am okay with your continuing to use it, but I recommend limiting its use to sleep time only — not during the day and not to pacify your baby if he is crying when awake.

Although I do like the dummy for young babies I think they can be overused — for example, when parents start to use them during the waking hours just to stop the baby whingeing or crying. A baby of this age cries or whinges for a reason, and so rather than popping a dummy in his mouth to keep him quiet you really need to investigate why your baby is not happy.

If the dummy has started to cause sleep problems overnight — and by that I mean if you are having to get up during the night just to put the dummy back in, and this is not when you are trying to stretch the feeding times — then I recommend getting rid of the dummy altogether. I know there will be some gasps of horror when you read this, but it is much easier to get rid of the dummy when your baby is younger rather than wait until he is older.

For a young baby — and I would wait until he is about four months old before getting rid of it — the best way of doing that is to just stop using it altogether. Use the Babybliss Settling Technique to get him back to sleep rather than the dummy.

Because your baby is young it won't take him long to get over the need for the dummy. If you persevere with not using it, it should take only a day or two for him to forget he ever had one.

If you are terrified of the thought of getting rid of it, and it is not really causing too many problems with your baby's sleep then keep using it. But I highly recommend that it is gone by the time your baby is six months old.

## CASE STUDY
### Emma

Emma was waking every two hours overnight to be fed. She was about three-and-a-half months when I first visited her and was not really in any kind of routine during the day — just being fed every two or three hours and being put down to sleep when her mother thought she was tired. That could be between three and five times a day. Emma's mum was getting frustrated and, although she wasn't really a 'routine person', she was beginning to think that maybe a routine would be a good thing to try.

As with most young babies who aren't sleeping as much as they should, Emma was really overtired and wound up. She was difficult to get to sleep and once asleep could sleep anywhere between 20 minutes and two hours — there was no established pattern. Another problem was that because she was so tired and up and down all day, when she fed she would only take enough to alleviate her hunger as she was too tired to really fill up and have a great feed. Often babies who catnap also snack when feeding and the behaviour becomes a bit of a cycle. They don't have enough milk in their tummy to help them sleep for long periods and because they don't sleep and are so tired they can only snack before falling asleep or giving up.

The first thing I did was give Emma's mum a routine to follow. The routine allowed for Emma to be up for one-and-a-half to two hours at a time and have three definite sleeps during the day. She was also to stay in her cot for as long as she was supposed to be asleep, and, if she woke before she was due to, her mum had to resettle her using the Babybliss Settling Technique. Overnight she was to have two feeds, one anywhere between 11 pm and 1 am, and the next one any time after 4 am. She then had to start her day around 7 am so her routine would not be thrown out. If she woke at 6 am that was fine, but no later than 7 am. Her parents were to use the settling technique overnight to get her back to sleep if she woke before she was due to feed. Emma's feeds were to be a minimum of three-hourly during the day and, if she needed it, she could have a cluster feed around 5 or 6 pm.

Although the first couple of nights were a bit difficult, the days started to sort themselves out almost as soon as Emma's mum implemented the routine. She did need to do some resettling occasionally but because Emma was now having big, focused feeds and plenty of activity in her up-time, she really took to sleeping longer. Overnight she quickly caught on to the two feeds as she was no longer so hungry.

Suffice to say, Emma's mum is now a 'routine person'!

## Sleeping summary

Between 12 and 18 weeks is the time to get a routine sorted. Remember routine and ritual are very important in your baby's life, and yours too. Be consistent with your rituals and start to implement a pattern and rhythm to your days.

You can also try to get your baby to sleep longer overnight, and you can work on getting him past being a catnapper during the day. The sooner the better, really. Also, consider getting rid of the dummy if you find you are getting up more often overnight than you have been previously just to put the dummy back in.

## Babybliss Settling Technique

Because using the Babybliss Settling Technique is very relevant to this age group, I am going to go through the whole process again in this section. It is usually at this age, too, that you may need to remove a sleep association or teach your baby to sleep better during the day and overnight. The Babybliss Settling Technique is a great alternative to the two extremes of settling babies: Controlled Crying and Attachment Parenting. I developed this technique while trying not to leave babies to cry but also wanting to teach them to self-settle without the use of any props, including a parent or care-giver. The idea behind the technique is to teach babies to feel comfortable about being in their own beds, and be able to calm themselves down and put themselves to sleep, both initially and throughout the night as they move through their sleep cycles.

The ideal time to start using this technique is when your baby is fairly young. By that I mean you can start whenever your baby starts to not sleep for as long as he is supposed to, day or night. In babies under three months, the technique is mostly used to get them past catnapping during their daytime sleeps. In older babies over six months, it is most often used to teach them to sleep all night.

So if your baby wakes before he is supposed to, go to him and commence settling. If he is a young baby who is still being wrapped, then ensure that he is still wrapped nice and tightly. If not, then rewrap him quickly and with him lying on his back pat him on the opposite shoulder to where you are standing. The pat needs to be rhythmical, at a slow-heartbeat pace. Continue patting until he has calmed down and, for the first couple of times it is a good idea to actually pat him off to sleep.

As well as patting him with him lying on his back, you can also try turning him on his side and patting him on his nappy. If the pat is not that effective or your baby is really upset and you have been patting for a while, then you can also rock your baby. By this I mean keep him in the cot and lying either on his back or on his side put one hand on his hip and the other on his shoulder and gently rock him from side to side. The rock can be quite fast and strong if he is upset but as he calms slow the rock down to a little jiggle.

After a couple of days of doing this try to work towards leaving the baby when he is calm and drowsy but still awake to let him do the last bit of going off to sleep on his own. As soon as he starts to cry, go to him and use the technique to calm him down but when he is calm, leave him to it.

If your baby is over six months of age and is waking overnight when he is not supposed to then the technique is almost the same except that if the baby is rolling and sleeping on his side or tummy then settle him in that position.

Again, for the first couple of nights you are doing this don't leave him when he is awake and crying, but stay with him until he is asleep. After a couple of nights, try to leave the room before he is sound asleep. It is also a good thing over the course of three nights to reduce the amount of rocking or patting you are doing so that you start rubbing his back rather than patting, and then just putting your hands on him rather than rocking. It is important to remember that the aim is for him to be doing most of the putting himself to sleep and not you.

If he does start to complain when you leave, give him the chance to calm himself down and go to sleep. But if after three to five minutes you feel he is winding up, then go to him and recommence the settling. For a young baby under six months of age, only leave him to cry for one to two minutes before going to him.

I find this technique is 100 per cent successful in teaching babies to sleep on their own but it can take anywhere from two nights to two weeks to be completely effective, and I have had the odd stubborn little baby who took a bit longer. But we have always got there in the end. Of course, a lot depends on you continuing with the technique and being consistent in the way you deal with your baby. Remember your baby *needs* time to learn and you are his teacher.

# Baby feeding

Your baby should still be exclusively milk-fed at this age. However, there are some parents who introduce solids around four months of age. I don't recommend that unless there is a medical reason for doing so. If your GP or paediatrician has advised you start feeding solids to your baby early then that is what you should do, but I follow the World Health Organization recommendation to exclusively milk-feed until six months of age.

## How often should I feed and how much does she need?

### *Breastfeeding*

If you are breastfeeding then you may still have to feed your baby every three hours during the day. This is absolutely fine if your baby still needs it. It is also a good idea to feed your baby more regularly during the day so she might sleep better overnight.

Your baby will increase the amount she takes from you as she grows and your breasts will increase their supply, so you shouldn't need to really worry too much about that. However if your baby is having a growth spurt then you might find that she wants to feed more frequently for a day or two. I would recommend feeding her frequently during the day and trying to stick with what you have been doing overnight. *Do not* introduce extra feeds at night when you haven't been doing them — as long as your baby is regularly gaining weight of course.

### Bottle-feeding

If you are bottle-feeding then you should be able to push your baby out to four-hourly feeds, if you haven't done so already. Most formula tins recommend the amount of milk to give the baby according to their age. But if you have a very big baby who finishes off her bottle at lightning speed, then it would be okay to increase the amount of formula to the next level to see if she needs a bit more.

You may also need to buy a faster teat size so she is getting the milk more quickly and won't be frustrated because it is too slow. By this age your baby should be on the fastest teat, but if you find that she is struggling or milk is running out the sides of her mouth then go back to the slower teat for another week or so.

Your baby should be down to two or even one feed per night, so she might be having only five to six feeds in a 24-hour period. As long as she is gaining weight steadily and is settled between feeds then that reduced number of feeds should be fine.

# Development and stimulation

By 12 to 18 weeks your baby has got the hang of being in the world. He is also getting to know you and you him. Your baby will be able to make lots of eye contact with you and almost seem like he can read your mood. If you are cross or look worried, he will look worried too. He has learnt that you are the most important person to him, the one who can meet his needs. He is, however, still not fully aware that he is a separate person from you.

Your baby will now be smiling back at you and laughing out loud with a gorgeous giggle. He will also start to smile and laugh at strangers because he has worked out that it is fun. He will start to 'chat' more with you and enjoy your conversations, making lots of sweet cooing and gurgling noises.

Babies at this age can get overstimulated easily as they seem to want to be engaged in activity more than they have before. It is worthwhile remembering that all the activity, conversation and play can easily turn him from a happy, contented baby to one who is overwhelmed by the world — he may start to cry, so he will need to be calmed. If this happens and you find yourself with a very tired and cranky baby, you will need to settle him by using the Babybliss Settling Technique (see pages 143–145).

## Developmental milestones

At this age your baby should be:

✦ smiling a lot

✦ laughing out loud and giggling

✦ becoming interested in people other than yourself

✦ a lot more interested in his surroundings and the outside world

✦ showing enjoyment in conversation and activities like bathing.

Physically, he will be progressing as well. He will start to have more control over his body and notice his hands and feet and touch and feel them, realising they are part of him. At this age he will begin to grasp at objects around him, occasionally grabbing them in his hands determined not to let go.

Tummy time is really good for your baby, the more practice he has lying on his tummy the better he will be at it. Tummy time is important because it helps babies strengthen their neck muscles and prepares them for crawling. It also helps them learn to push up on their arms, roll over and eventually sit up and stand. More recently it has been found that it also helps babies to get off their backs, lessening the pressure on their heads that can cause a flattening or misshaping of their heads. At first he may look like a beached swimmer, arms and legs flapping back and forth but not getting anywhere, and he may not like it, complaining after a short time, but if you give him about five to ten minutes every day he will start to enjoy his funny swimming time. Make sure there are things for him to look at or try to reach out to — this can distract him and makes his time extra fun. He may start to roll from his front to his back around four months, which is a very exciting milestone.

## Playing with your baby

Some things you can do to entertain and stimulate your baby at this age are:

+ reading stories while showing him the pictures in the book
+ making faces and playing peekaboo
+ singing songs and playing music to him
+ providing lots of brightly coloured objects for him to look at and things he can grasp
+ allowing nappy-free time on a mat on the floor, remembering to lie him on a towel or something absorbent to catch any little leakages
+ putting him under a baby gym with lots of hanging bright and noisy objects for him to grasp and hit.

# Chapter 7

# A little person: 18 weeks to six months

# Baby sleeping

By now you would be about ready to get some more sleep yourself, yes? If your baby is not already sleeping through the night, we need to get her to at least be sleeping through most of it.

Up until now she has probably been having two feeds overnight, one late in the evening and one early in the morning. If she isn't doing this yet, now is the time to work on it. Unless your baby is underweight, she really should be able to last overnight with just the two feeds, the late evening one and the early morning one.

Until the baby is on solids it is an unreasonable expectation for her to sleep for 11 or 12 hours overnight without a feed. I am discussing this age as if your baby is not eating solids yet and so still needs those couple of night feeds. But as I outlined in the last section (see pages 137–139), you really need to get her feeding at the beginning and the end of the night, not in the middle. So read that section again if you haven't reached that stage.

## When should my baby sleep and for how long?

You will notice that your baby is increasingly more alert and wanting to stay up for longer periods between sleeps during the day, and by six months she should be able to stay awake for about two to two-and-a-half hours at a time. At the beginning of the day you might find she gets tired pretty quickly, but I encourage you to try to keep your baby up for at least 90 minutes before putting her back to bed.

Overnight, at this age your baby should be sleeping for about 11 to 12 hours with one to two feeds and these should be in the late evening, around 10.30 to 11 pm and the early morning, around 5 am. If your baby has dropped the late evening feed, she will probably be waking anywhere between 4 and 5 am for a feed and then be up for the day at 6.30 to 7 am. If you are one of those lucky parents whose baby has dropped all the night feeds and is sleeping through, then that's fantastic.

You still need to watch your baby for tired signs and also make sure you have one eye on the clock so you are not keeping her up for too long. Remember, an overtired baby can find it much harder to go off to sleep and may need lots of intervention from you. So it is in both of your interests to get her to bed before she is too tired.

At this age tired signs include:

✦ grizzling or crying
✦ clenching of the fists
✦ grimacing
✦ yawning

◆ rubbing the eyes or face

◆ pulling at the ears.

In summary:

| Age | Up-time | Down-time | Average sleeps |
| --- | --- | --- | --- |
| 18 weeks | 1½ to 2 hours | 1½ to 2½ hours | Three definite day sleeps: two long and one shorter, and 11 to 12 hours overnight with one to two feeds. |
| 6 months | 2 to 2½ hours | 1½ to 2½ hours | Three definite day sleeps: two long and one shorter, and 11 to 12 hours overnight with one to two feeds. |

## Babybliss routine and ritual

At this age routine is really important and a great benefit for both you and your baby. If you are struggling with getting your baby into a good routine then I really encourage you to try to set one now. Of course, you don't have to be rigidly strict with the times, but each day should follow the same pattern if possible, give or take 30 minutes.

A good routine for a baby of this age would be as follows:

| | |
|---|---|
| 4.30 to 5 am | Breastfeed or bottle-feed then straight back to sleep. (Note: if your baby sleeps through to 6 am it is okay to start the day then.) |
| 6.30 to 7 am | Up for the day. Babies should have some activity, then a feed, then some more activity and then be put back to bed. This cycle should last no longer than about 2 hours. |
| Around 8.30 to 9 am | Morning sleep. This sleep should last about 2 hours but can be between 1½ and 3 hours. |
| 10 to 10.30 am | Up from sleep. Repeat the activity/feed/activity cycle. This cycle can last from 2 to 2½ hours for this age. |
| 12 to 12.30 pm | Put baby down for the midday sleep. This sleep should last about 2 hours but can be between 1½ and 3 hours. |

| | |
|---|---|
| Around 2 pm | Up from sleep. Repeat the activity/feed/activity cycle. This cycle can last from 2 to 2½ hours for a baby close to six months. |
| 4 pm | Put baby down for the afternoon sleep. This nap is usually a shorter nap and may only last for 30 to 45 minutes as your baby gets older. This shorter time is okay as this nap will be dropped around six months. |
| 4.30 to 5 pm | Up from sleep. Don't let your baby sleep past 5 pm as you really want him to go to bed for the night at around 6.30 to 7 pm at the latest. He won't be tired enough if he slept too late in the afternoon. |
| 6 to 7 pm | Bedtime ritual. This can include a bath, more quiet activity like a story, then a feed and then into bed. This ritual needs to be the same every night. |

## Getting rid of sleep associations

By six months of age you really want your baby to be completely self-settling — that is, putting herself to sleep initially and then back to sleep if she wakes before she is due to get up. So now is the time to break all those habits and props you have been using to get her to sleep and stay asleep. She needs to learn to do it on her own so she can put herself back to sleep overnight once you stop the night feeding.

It is a great thing to teach a baby to self-settle. Of all the things that happen to a baby, being able to put herself to sleep is really the first thing she can learn to do on her own. Once she has learnt how to self-settle she won't need you to help her get off to sleep, which is a great development stage.

So look at what associations she uses to go to sleep. By that I mean what you have been doing to get her off to sleep. And that could include such things as using the dummy, rocking her in your arms, feeding her off to sleep, putting her in your bed, feeding her overnight when she doesn't need it, walking her up and down the hallway, pushing her in the pram, driving her in the car and countless other measures.

These associations and props usually start from when your baby is quite young. You may have used something that worked a treat and so you have kept on using it every time you put your baby to bed because you know it will work. Don't feel bad about that, most babies under 12 weeks of age cannot self-settle and need you to help them get off to sleep. But it is when they can *only* go off to sleep with all these conditions in place that it becomes a problem.

Around five or six months of age, babies' sleep cycles change, their sleep may become more disturbed and they can start to wake more often than they have previously. I often hear from parents that they had a baby who was a great sleeper, and then all of a sudden, out of the blue, that changed. The baby started waking more frequently overnight. What can then happen is that the parents are really perplexed and introduce something new, like feeding their baby more often, or picking her up to rock her, or putting the baby into their bed, just to get her back to sleep, hoping that this little problem will pass. But babies are creatures of habit and you only need to do something new to a baby to get her to sleep twice — especially when they aren't doing the work — and it will become the baby's new association. So you are now in a bind, having to do this new thing in order for her to go back to sleep. And, as she is now a bit older and everyone wants to get some more sleep, you keep reinforcing this association and she will find it more and more difficult to go off to sleep without it.

## The dummy

If your baby is still using a dummy then you will probably find that you have been getting up more and more overnight to put that dummy back in your baby's mouth. There are some babies who aren't bothered if the dummy falls out, but they are rare. Because babies are unable to put the dummy back in their mouth at this age I recommend getting rid of it altogether.

I know a lot of parents will be horrified by that suggestion as they probably use the dummy as a bit of a crutch themselves — that is, you know that if your baby won't go off to sleep you can put the dummy in and off she goes. But you will find that once you get rid of the dummy her sleep will improve greatly both during the day and at night.

So how do you get rid of the dummy? There are two ways: cold turkey and gradual. I actually favour the 'cold turkey' method because it doesn't prolong the process and at this age your baby will forget she ever had a dummy in a couple of days. I also don't think going cold turkey is any more distressing for the baby, in fact I think it is better to get it over with quickly. But some parents don't want to do it that way, and that is absolutely fine too.

To use the 'cold turkey' method, firstly you have to throw out all the dummies in the house so you won't be tempted to use one. Make sure there are none lurking in the car or the pram either. I know there have been times when desperate mums and dads have searched the house looking for a stray dummy. I recommend you start the process when you put the baby down for the night, because at this time you know she will go off to sleep eventually. So just put her down in her cot as you normally would but without the dummy. If she is really addicted to the dummy she will start to complain and then cry as she gets frustrated and tired. Once she has started to cry you should go to her and use the Babybliss Settling Technique to get her off to sleep. Pat her as you would when she was younger, until she goes to sleep. If she stops crying and is calm then you can leave her to go off to sleep, but I recommend that you stay with her until she is asleep. The patting needs to reflect the crying, so the more upset she is the faster you pat. Once she starts to calm then you slow down the patting. When her eyes close stop patting, but leave your hands on her until she is asleep. You should also be shooshing the whole time you are settling her. Once she is asleep you can leave the room. You need to repeat this same settling process if she wakes overnight.

The 'gradual' method of removing the dummy is essentially the same, but you can still use it as a last resort for the first three to five nights. For example, if you have been doing the settling for 30 minutes or so, give her the dummy just to get her off to sleep. The dummy is only used if she has not gone to sleep or back to sleep after 30 minutes or so of the settling. Repeat this for three nights, then for the next three nights don't use the dummy unless she has not gone back to sleep after 45 minutes. Keep extending the time without the dummy by 15 minutes every three or so nights.

You should find that after about 24 to 48 hours of no dummy at all, whether you use the cold turkey or the gradual method, that your baby will have forgotten that she ever had one and her sleep will be much more settled.

### The wrap or swaddle

Once your baby has started to roll, which happens at five or six months of age, you need to stop wrapping her at sleep times. Once she is rolling, if she is still being wrapped she will wake because she now needs to move around and reposition herself in her sleep, just like we do. Wrapping a baby at this age may still be the trigger to get her off to sleep and be part of the sleeping ritual, but if you continue relying on this, you will have to get up overnight to either rewrap her or to settle her when she wakes.

The method for removing the wrap is essentially the same as for removing the dummy. And there are also the same two ways of doing it: cold turkey or the gradual method.

Again, I recommend that you get rid of it quickly rather than prolonging the whole thing as I don't believe it is any more distressing for the baby, but some people prefer to do it gradually and that is okay. When you stop using the wrap I recommend that you replace it with a sleeping bag. A sleeping bag is a fantastic sleep aid. It keeps the baby covered all night so she doesn't get too hot or too cold, and it can be incorporated into the bedtime ritual so it replaces the wrap as the trigger for sleep — that is, every time the baby is put into the sleeping bag she knows she is going to bed.

So if you intend to go cold turkey on the wrap, put them all away somewhere, put her into a sleeping bag and continue with the usual bedtime ritual. Once again I recommend starting this at the night-time bedtime as you will be assured that she will eventually go off to sleep, although it may take her a bit longer than usual.

Once she is in bed, use the Babybliss Settling Technique to get her off to sleep. It will probably take her longer to go to sleep than she is used to because all of a sudden her arms are out and flailing, and she can get her hands in her mouth. So you will have to persevere until she has gone to sleep the first time you make the change and once you have got her off to sleep a couple of times without the wrap she will not remember that she ever used it.

If you want to remove the wrap gradually, then I recommend you start wrapping her with one arm out. Do this for three days and use the settling technique if necessary to get her off to sleep. Then for the next three nights wrap her with both arms out and again use the settling technique if you need to. After six nights, put her in a sleeping bag and see how she goes, obviously using the settling technique to get her off to sleep if she is struggling a bit. This pattern of days is flexible, so if you feel she needs more time with one or both arms out before you remove the wrap, then be guided by her behaviour. Again, because she now has more control over her arms, it won't take her long to get used to not being in the wrap.

### Rocking, patting and picking up

A lot of babies will be used to being put to sleep in their parents' arms, in a rocker, in the pram (that is being pushed) or in other ways rather than in their own cot. You now need to teach your baby how to fall asleep in her cot. I know this can be daunting as most of you have tried to get your baby to go to sleep in her cot but there has been a lot of crying and resistance on the baby's part. I want you to know that it is really very easy to get your baby to like sleeping in her cot and to be able to fall asleep there.

When I visit parents who have been struggling with this, they feel overwhelmed that their baby just won't ever go off to sleep, so after trying to settle their baby in the cot for a bit they give up and go back to doing what they have found worked in the past. This problem can be worse during the day sleeps, when a lot of babies protest about sleeping in their bed for their daytime naps but are okay to go down at night. If this is the case then you have to really work on those daytime sleeps. If it is all the sleeps that are a problem, or particularly the nights, then start the new routine when you are putting her down at the end of the day.

The method is the same as the one used for teaching her to sleep without aids and to self-settle. Put her down for her sleep in her cot. Of course she will not like this as she is usually asleep when she is put to bed, so she will express her dislike by crying, which is her way of protesting. Rest assured that she will go to sleep eventually. A lot of the fear in changing things with babies is that parents don't know what the outcome will be — will the baby ever go to sleep again? — so they are afraid to change. Or they have tried and the baby was distressed and crying and they weren't sure if she would ever stop crying and go to sleep, so they abandoned the new way and went back to the old tried-and-tested way of her going off to sleep. Well I assure you that she will *always* stop crying and she will *always* go off to sleep if you deal with everything in a gentle way. Use the Babybliss Settling Technique outlined throughout this book to get her to go to sleep in her cot.

If it is a daytime sleep then it might take some time to get her there and you really need to stay with her, patting and calming her until she is sound asleep. If it is at night-time then you may

163

find it is a bit easier, or it could be a bit harder — there are no hard and fast rules here. The key to your success in getting her to sleep is to stick with it, settling her till she goes to sleep.

Caring for a baby is really so much about consistency, and so when you are teaching your baby something new you have to repeat the new process over and over, the same way every time, in order for her to get the hang of it. If you think about it, this is the way babies and children learn everything. So it is completely up to you, as your baby's teachers, to show her the new way of going to sleep, and also give her time to learn it. I know some people who start the new technique and then give up because it isn't working quickly enough or their baby is really resisting and struggling to go off to sleep. But it is kinder to stick with it until it is done, otherwise your baby will become more and more confused and not be sure of what is expected of her when she is put to bed. And when a baby is confused her behaviour and sleep becomes more and more erratic.

## Catnapping

At this age some babies can still be catnappers during the day. This is not great as by now you would hope that they are getting their three day sleeps, two that are about one-and-a-half hours to two hours long and the other one being anywhere from 40 to 60 minutes.

If your baby is still waking after one sleep cycle then I would suggest you go back to the previous section (see pages 114–118) and follow the technique for dealing with catnapping. The sooner you get the catnapping sorted the better as your baby is still very young and can easily pick up new sleep habits.

## CASE STUDY
### Edie

One problem at this age is those babies who won't sleep anywhere else other than in the baby carrier or the pram for their day sleeps. And because of this, they will only sleep for one sleep cycle. I went to see a gorgeous little girl named Edie whose mother was beside herself because Edie would only have her day sleeps in the baby carrier. This meant that Edie's mum was spending a lot of her day wandering the streets with her, hoping that Edie would sleep. When she was little this method was successful but now that Edie was close to six months old it was taking longer and longer for her to go off to sleep and, when she did, she would only stay asleep for 30 minutes. The whole process had become difficult for both Mum and Edie.

I told her mum we were going to put Edie down for her day sleep awake and use the Babybliss Settling Technique to get her off to sleep. At the first sleep Edie was very distressed as she had never gone to sleep in her cot during the day. Getting her off to sleep didn't take as long as I thought it would and after about 15 minutes she went to sleep. Miraculously, she slept for close to two hours — she hadn't ever slept that long during the day, even when she was little. Her mum was amazed. At her second sleep it took less time to get Edie off to sleep, about six minutes, and then again she slept for close to two hours.

Edie took to her new sleep routine immediately, and her mum reported to me that from that first day onwards Edie slept really well at both sleeps. She was very easy to put down and there was no crying after about three days. Everyone was very happy!

## Sleeping summary

This age is a bit of a milestone in terms of sleep. Things seem to change around the five to six month mark and babies' sleep can either get better or worse. It is important to remember not to introduce anything new and use the settling technique to get over any abnormal wakes during the night. This is also a good time to get rid of any sleep associations and get your routine really happening.

The main things to remember when changing a sleep habit or removing props are:

✦ be consistent
✦ repeat, repeat and repeat the new process
✦ use the settling technique to get your baby to sleep
✦ stick with it until your baby has gone to sleep.

# Baby feeding

You may discover that around this age, five to six months, your baby seems to be more interested in what you are eating. You may even see him opening his little mouth in anticipation that you are going to put some of your food in it. This is one of the signs that your baby is nearing the age when he will start solids. However, because the World Health Organization's guideline is to not feed your baby solids until he is six months of age, I will discuss introducing solids in the next chapter.

If you have already introduced solids to your baby or are thinking about doing it, then that is completely your decision. There are some instances where the baby needs to start solids a little bit earlier. I recommend, however, that you seek advice from a health professional about starting early rather than taking advice solely from friends or family members, who of course, only have your baby's best interests at heart.

## How much should I feed and how much does he need?

*Breastfeeding*

If you are breastfeeding then by this age you will have noticed that your baby has completely mastered the feeding and is able to finish off a feed at lightning speed. Some mothers worry that because their baby is feeding so quickly — in some cases the feed can be over in ten minutes flat — that the baby isn't getting enough milk. As long as the baby seems satisfied at the end of the feed, and he is sleeping well and gaining weight, then he will be getting plenty of milk.

Babies can also become increasingly distracted while they are feeding, pulling off regularly to look around or if you are talking they will pull off to watch you talk. If this is happening and you are worried that your baby isn't feeding well because he is so distracted, then take him into a quiet room, away from the noise of the TV or other people and finish the feed there. Some babies just want you to themselves while they are feeding and will feed better when it is just you and him, and nothing else.

At this age you can also have a better idea of when the feeds will happen, although you may still be feeding three-hourly during the day, which is fine. However, if your baby is not really that interested or becoming increasingly distracted and only snacking at feeds, then try to stretch him out to four-hourly feeds. If not at every feed, then at least for a couple during the day.

If you are exclusively breastfeeding your baby then it is hard to know how much he is getting, but as long as he seems settled after the feed, is sleeping well and gaining weight routinely then he should be getting enough milk.

If your baby is sleeping all night and having good sleeps during the day then you may only be able to get four feeds into him every 24 hours and that is absolutely fine if he is gaining weight. I had one baby who started to sleep through very early and was such a great sleeper during the day that his mum could only feed him four times and occasionally only three. He was not on solids but was a big, thriving boy and so was obviously getting plenty of milk when he did feed.

Again, you need to take into consideration genetics when you are looking at your baby's weight gain and size. If you are big people, or one of you is particularly tall, then your baby may be bigger than other babies at the same age. The same goes if you are a small woman and you have a little girl baby who is not as big as other babies in your mothers' group but if she is happy and gaining weight steadily there is nothing to worry about. Always look at your baby as an individual. I know it is hard not to compare your baby with other babies but when you are doing that make sure you look at yourselves as well.

## Bottle-feeding

If you are bottle-feeding your baby, the same thing can be happening with your baby becoming distracted when feeding. If that is the case, then you may need to give him the bottle in a quiet place away from a lot of distraction. He should also be taking a bit more from the bottle now, so if he is becoming a bit unsettled or waking overnight when he shouldn't be, increase the amount he is taking in the bottle.

The standard calculation for how much a baby should be getting to drink is 150 millilitres per kilogram per day. So you need to take into consideration how much your baby weighs when working out how much formula to give him. The tin will have a guideline on how much you should give, but if you have a really big baby or a little baby then you can use that calculation to help you give him what he needs.

At this age you could be feeding your baby every four hours if you aren't already. But if you find he won't last or you are worried about his weight gain then three-hourly feeding is okay during the day although the ideal would definitely be down to two feeds overnight.

# Development and stimulation

Between 18 weeks and six months your baby's development can seem to just take off. He is really starting to engage with you and others, such as giggling and laughing a lot and making lots of noises that sound like he is trying to communicate with you. He also listens to what you have to say to him and really tries hard to mimic you, so it is a great idea to repeat words and sounds over and over again, like 'ma ma' or 'da da'. It is also a good time to repeat his name to him over and over, and he will begin to respond to it when you say it.

At this age your baby will stick his tongue out at you if you stick your tongue out at him and will turn and look towards where sounds are coming from. He will also recognise voices and familiar sounds and turn towards them when he hears them. He will follow objects and people with his eyes and can focus on small objects.

You will also notice that your baby is grabbing and holding onto objects and putting almost everything in his mouth. Physically, he will be rolling over from his front onto his back and may even have mastered the roll from back to front and the complete 360-degree roll.

## Developmental milestones

Always remember that babies do things at their own pace, so try not to compare your baby with another baby. But if you are worried about your baby's development and he hasn't met his milestones, then it is worthwhile to get him seen by your GP or a paediatrician. At this age your baby will:

+ grasp objects when they are placed in his hands
+ roll over onto his side (by about five months)
+ start to react to familiar situations by cooing and smiling, and kicking his arms and legs with excitement
+ babble a lot and take his turn when speaking
+ turn his head to look at who is speaking.

**Playing with your baby**

Some things you can do to entertain and stimulate your baby at this age are:

+ talk to your baby and always tell him what you are doing
+ repeat sounds and play word games with him
+ make faces and play peekaboo
+ put him on his tummy to play on the floor to encourage him to get used to being on his tummy when he rolls onto it

- ✦ play music and sing to him
- ✦ have lots of brightly coloured toys nearby so he can touch and explore them by putting them in his mouth
- ✦ sit on the floor with him 'sitting' between your legs and read to him or play with toys that make noises.

# Teething

There are hundreds of theories on teething, when it happens and how it affects the baby. Whatever anyone says about teething, when that first little tooth appears in your baby's mouth is a very exciting milestone.

To reach the complete set of baby teeth takes about the first three years of your child's life. First teeth start to appear any time between three and twelve months but it usually is around six months that you notice the first little tooth break through. The first teeth to appear are usually the lower central incisors and the last are the upper and lower second molars at the back of the mouth.

Teething is often associated with some not so pleasant symptoms. These can start early, around three months, and go on for months and months until a tooth appears. Some of the symptoms of teething include:

✦ drooling, which can be excessive

✦ swollen and reddened gums

✦ biting down on objects

✦ pain and irritability.

Some people suggest that babies can also get red cheeks, diarrhoea and a fever with teething but most experts agree that these are *not* teething symptoms and that your baby might actually be sick, so it is advisable to get her checked out by your GP if this is the case. Although I have seen babies get those kinds of symptoms when they are teething, if your baby has a temperature then I recommend checking for other things that might be going on. You will also hear some people say that they don't believe teething affects babies at all and something else is causing your baby to be unsettled.

I believe teething *can* be upsetting for babies. I have seen babies who refuse to have spoons, teats or dummies put in their mouth, and I have seen babies with swollen gums who are miserable. So I am a firm believer that teething can be a painful experience for some babies. But often teething can be attributed to many events or behaviours in a baby when that is just not the case. If a mother asks me if teething is causing her baby to wake overnight, I ask her a few questions:

◆ Is the baby's behaviour normal and happy during
    the day?
◆ Is she taking her milk and solids as she normally would?
◆ Are her daytime sleeps the same as they have
    always been?

If the answer is yes to these questions then I would deduce that teething is not the cause of whatever issue the baby is having. It is important to remember that teething doesn't occur only at night.

Teething is a 24-hour event, so if your baby is behaving normally and is happy and sleeping as she usually does during the day then it shouldn't be teething that is upsetting her at night.

If her behaviour is different during the day, then it could be the teething that is the culprit for the different behaviour. There are a number of things you can do to help your baby get through her bout of teething.

Teething rings are beneficial, especially if they are the type that can be put in the fridge to make them cold. The coldness soothes the baby's inflamed gums and relieves the pain. If your baby is on solids, she might get some relief from cold foods rather than warm. Cold puréed fruit or jelly are usually good at these times. If she is in real distress you can give her an infant pain relief medication, but make sure to consult the bottle for the correct dose for her age.

Remember, if your baby is inconsolable, has a temperature, diarrhoea or is generally unwell then you should consult your GP before assuming that it is simply teething problems.

## Stages of teething

All babies will get their teeth at different times, and although the timing may be slightly different teething does follow the same pattern.

### Stage 1

Teething starts well before the teeth appear. Babies are born with 20 teeth hidden underneath the gums. You can often see a white nodule-like appearance on the gum where the tooth is about to erupt, or feel where the teeth will come through if you run a finger over your baby's gums.

### Stage 2

Somewhere between six and 12 months the first four front teeth will appear. These are the incisor teeth. The bottom two usually appear first, followed by the top two.

### Stage 3

Molar teeth will usually appear anywhere from between 12 and 18 months. The first molars to appear are usually behind the canine teeth.

### Stage 4

The canine teeth usually appear somewhere between 16 months and 22 months. Sometimes the molars can appear before the canine teeth.

### Stage 5

The second molars usually appear between two and three years of age. These are the largest teeth and the last ones to arrive. They can also cause quite a bit of disruption in your toddler's behaviour as they can be painful.

|         | Age                        | Teeth                                                                                                          |
| ------- | -------------------------- | ------------------------------------------------------------------------------------------------------------ |
| Stage 1 | From birth                 | 20 teeth sit under the gums. They can be felt or seen as a white nodule on the gum.                           |
| Stage 2 | Between six and 12 months  | First four teeth will appear. Bottom two first, then top two.                                                 |
| Stage 3 | Between 12 and 18 months   | Molar teeth will start to appear. The first molars to appear are usually are behind the canine teeth.        |
| Stage 4 | Between 16 and 22 months   | The canine teeth start to appear. Molars can appear before the canines.                                       |
| Stage 5 | Between two and three years | The second molars will appear.                                                                               |

# Chapter 8

# Becoming more mobile: six to nine months

# Baby sleeping

Between six and nine months your baby should be in an established routine and sleeping well both day and night. If you are still feeding overnight then now is the time you can start to reduce that and hopefully by nine months have a baby who is sleeping all night — that is, 11 to 12 hours every night. During the day, at around six months, your baby will reduce his daytime naps down to two per day, totalling about three to three-and-a-half hours sleep in total.

Hopefully you will have eliminated most if not all of the sleep associations that you may have been using to get your baby to go to sleep and stay asleep. If this is not the case then I would recommend that you reread pages 156–164 and implement the techniques outlined there so you can get to the point where your baby is sleeping well with little intervention from you.

The process is the same for all babies under the age of 18 months. The only difference would be if your baby is rolling in his cot at night, which means that you need to settle him where he is. For example, if he is sleeping on his side or tummy, don't keep flipping him over onto his back. If your baby is rolling around on his own then it is safe for him to sleep where he ends up — as long as there is nothing in his cot that he could get caught under. This is why I recommend the use of a sleeping bag once your baby is out of his wrap. That way you can remove all the bedding and he should be safe to move about the cot without getting stuck under anything.

## Sleep cycles

It is around the age of six months that babies' sleep cycles change slightly and they start to sleep more like we do. Their sleep cycles become slightly longer and the way they sleep overnight is in a pattern. That is, they have their deepest sleep of the night in the hours before midnight. It usually takes babies about 20 minutes to get into that deep sleep after they are put to bed. Once they are in that deep sleep they can have a short arousal after about 45 minutes but then they stay in their deep sleep until around midnight. So babies who wake in these hours are reasonably easy to resettle, although there are always exceptions.

Between midnight and 5 am they have their dream sleep or rapid eye movement (REM) sleep. This is the time when they can be quite restless and will move around the cot. If they are waking at night, these are the hours they will be awake the most as they are never really in a deep sleep.

Around 5 am they go back into their second deep sleep of the night. Babies need to have this second deep sleep and not start the day at 5 am. If they do get up to start the day without having this deep sleep, they will be really tired for the first part of the day. Most parents will then put them back to bed early in the morning and they will finish off their night sleep then, often sleeping for at least 90 minutes. If you continue to do this, you will encourage the baby to keep waking around 5 am and not want to go back to sleep. So although a lot of babies will be wakeful around 5 am as they move out of their REM sleep, they need to go back to sleep for at least another hour.

## When should my baby sleep and for how long?

From around six months of age your baby should be able to stay awake for two to two-and-a-half hours at a time during the day, and by nine months she should be able to stay awake for up to three hours at a time. It is important to know that as your baby grows she does need to be awake longer and burn up more energy when she is awake in order for her to be tired enough to have good solid daytime sleeps. So as well as noticing the tired signs, you should also keep one eye on the clock. I do not mean that you should keep your baby awake till she is beside herself with tiredness because, as we all know, an overtired baby will not sleep well. But if you have a baby who has always only been up for 90 minutes before she has been put down to sleep, her little body clock will start to make her feel tired at the 90-minute mark because that is what she has always done. I recommend you start to stretch this out by 15 minutes every three days, so she can slowly get used to staying up longer and she won't be desperate with tiredness.

At six months, or thereabouts, your baby will drop from three daytime sleeps to two daytime sleeps. To help her with this development you drop the late-afternoon sleep and because she is able to be awake a bit longer between sleeps, the second sleep moves to later in the afternoon. When you do drop down to two sleeps it means that the time between her waking from her second sleep and the time she goes to bed for the night can be quite long, but as this time of the day is usually busy with dinner, bath and so on, you will be able to distract her with enough activity to get her through to bedtime without too much fuss. You can also bring her bedtime forward a bit, to about 6.15 or 6.30 pm if she is really struggling, just until she gets used to being awake longer.

You also may find that as your baby grows she starts to have one shorter sleep and one longer sleep during the day. This is absolutely fine and normal but I recommend that she has the shorter sleep in the morning and her longer sleep after lunch. This is so the afternoon is not too long for her and also because the second sleep, or the midday sleep, is the one she will keep when she moves to one sleep per day, so it is the most important sleep. When that happens, you want that middle-of-the-day sleep to be a long one. If your baby is having a big first sleep and a shorter second sleep, then the way to change her daytime sleeps is to wake her from her morning sleep after about 60 minutes, and keep her up until she is due to go down again. Do not put her down earlier than you normally would, and hopefully she will have a big second sleep. If she is used to sleeping for only one sleep cycle, you may need to resettle her for a couple of days until she gets the hang of sleeping longer at that time. So in summary:

| Age | Up-time | Down-time | Average sleeps |
|-----|---------|-----------|----------------|
| 6 months | 2 to 2½ hours | 1½ to 2 hours | Drops down to two daytime sleeps totalling about 3 to 3½ hours, 11 to 12 hours per night. |
| 9 months | 2½ to 3 hours | 1½ to 2 hours | Two definite day sleeps totalling about 3 hours, 11 to 12 hours per night. |

## How do I drop the night feeds?

If you are still feeding your baby overnight — and hopefully it is only once or twice, usually a late night feed and an early morning feed — then now is the time to introduce solid food and reduce those night feeds. I can hear the cheers already!

Once he starts on solids then I recommend you first drop the late evening feed. Of course, this is only if you are still doing that feed. If you aren't doing a late evening feed then obviously you don't have to worry about this. When you have started introducing solids, make sure she is happily taking one to two meals per day and then start to skip the first night feed.

To do that is really just the same process as if you were getting rid of an association or a bad habit (see page 156). When the baby wakes for that feed, rather than feeding her you resettle her back to sleep using the Babybliss Settling Technique. When you hear her cry, wait a couple of minutes then go into her. Settle her in whatever position she is in — that is, if she is on her side or her tummy then leave her there and settle her in that position. If she is in an awkward position then move her to the centre of the cot but place her in whatever position she prefers to sleep in. Put one hand on her shoulder or her upper back, if she is lying on her side or her tummy, and pat her nappy with the other hand.

> I always pat with the base of my hand and I pat in an upward motion so that I am almost rocking the baby slightly as well as patting.

The patting needs to reflect the crying from the baby, so the harder she is crying the faster you pat. You should also be shooshing her while you pat. If she is very loud then say the words 'Shoosh, shoosh', in a singsong manner so she can hear you over her crying. Singing or humming a lullaby or a familiar song can soothe her also and calm her if she is really upset.

Continue patting like this until your baby starts to calm down. If she gets really upset, then you can try alternating patting with rocking her from side to side, but always keeping her in the cot. Only pick her up if she has been crying for a long period (over 10 to 15 minutes) and the crying doesn't seem to be easing at all. Sometimes a baby can get herself into a crying phase that she doesn't seem to know how to stop. To calm her down and stop the crying, pick her up and calm her in your arms by patting her or gently rocking her. But the key is to not let her fall asleep in your arms. Once she has calmed, put her back in the cot for another couple of minutes. She will start to cry again but then you recommence the settling. Because she has been calmed and the crying cycle has been broken, it shouldn't take her too long to calm down in her cot.

As she starts to calm you can slow the patting right down. Keep doing this slow pat, at a heartbeat pace, along with saying a long 'shooooooosh' until she closes her eyes. When she has closed her eyes, stop patting but rub her back instead. Then stop rubbing but keep your hands on her. After a couple of minutes of doing this, and if you think she is asleep, then you can remove your hands but stay by the cot shooshing her for just another minute before leaving the room. If she starts to cry again after you leave wait about three to five minutes, depending on the intensity of the cry, before going back in and start the settling again.

It usually only takes one to two nights to get a baby to sleep past that first wake, but you may find that she will start to wake a bit earlier than she used to at the second wake. For example, she used to be fed at 11 pm and 5 am but after you dropped the 11 pm feed she started to wake at 3 am. My recommendation for this would be to use the settling technique to get her back to sleep but have a cut-off time. So, say, you will resettle till 4.30 am and then if she is still awake feed her. The aim is to get her as close to that early morning feed time as she was doing previously.

Once your baby is on full solids then you can definitely try to push her through the whole night. I recommend waiting until a baby has been on three meals a day for a couple of weeks, and even then you might find that she really can't get past 5 am without having a feed. It is reasonable for a baby to have that early morning feed for a little while, even until she is about nine months old. But you would definitely want to have dropped it by that age. To do that you employ exactly the same technique as you did for the late evening feed. It should only take around three nights to get her sleeping straight through to anywhere after 6 am.

## Babybliss routine and ritual

As we have discussed elsewhere, routine and ritual are really important for you and your baby. If you still haven't established a routine then I would recommend you start to implement one now and stick to it. At this age you can be more structured and really stick to set times of the day, especially for naps. At this age most babies respond well to having their day naps at the same time every day.

As babies get older they really respond to a nice routine. With a pattern to their day babies can be a bit more predictable and you will know what is happening from one day to the next. A good routine for a baby of this age would be as follows (the routine includes when you would feed solids once you have introduced them):

| | |
|---|---|
| 4.30 to 5.30 am | Breastfeed or bottle-feed then back to sleep. (Note: if your baby sleeps through then it is okay to give the milk feed at 6 to 6.30 am and then give breakfast any time after 7 am.) |
| 6 to 6.30 am | Up for the day. |
| 7 to 7.30 am | Breakfast. |
| 8 to 8.30 am | Breastfeed or bottle-feed if she hasn't had one since she got up for the day. |
| 8.30 to 9 am | Morning sleep. This sleep can be between 1 and 1½ hours. |
| 10 to 10.30 am | Up from sleep. |
| 11 am | Breastfeed or bottle-feed. When the baby has woken from her morning sleep, keep her up for about 15 minutes or so before offering her a feed so she doesn't associate waking up with being fed. |
| 12 pm | Lunch. |
| 1 pm to 1.30 pm | Afternoon sleep. This sleep should be between 1½ and 2 hours. |
| 3 to 3.30 pm | Up from sleep. |

| | |
|---|---|
| 3.30 to 4 pm | Breastfeed or bottle-feed. Some babies between six and nine months still need a milk feed around this time while they are getting used to solids and less day sleep. This feed can be stopped by nine months. |
| 5 pm | Dinner. |
| 5.30 to 6 pm | Bathtime. |
| 6 to 6.30 pm | Breastfeed or bottle-feed. |
| 6.30 to 7 pm | Bedtime. |

## Sleeping problems

Because this age can be a transitional time in a baby's development, his sleep can be disrupted. As well as waking overnight there can be the early morning wakes, any time from 4.30 am. This is due to the sleep cycles (see page 181) and it is important to get him back to sleep at this time. Babies have an internal body clock just like we do, and so if you are consistently getting your baby up to start the day at 5 am his body clock will just naturally adjust to this time and continue to wake him early.

There are, however, a small number of babies who are early-morning risers, and that there is nothing you can do to get them past that 5 to 5.30 am wake-up. But I do try everything possible to get a baby to sleep longer in the morning before I decide that he is an early riser and there is nothing that can be done about it. I recommend trying all you can to get your baby to get back to sleep, by using the settling technique and making sure you are not putting him back to bed for his morning nap any earlier than 8.30 am, before you give up and have to start your day early.

### *My baby used to sleep well but now he doesn't*

Six months can be a milestone time in a baby's life as lots of things are changing. Around six months his sleep cycles become longer than they were and he is also becoming much more mobile, perhaps even starting to sit up and move himself around a bit more. He is also starting solids and may be getting teeth. All these things can affect a baby's sleep.

I often get calls from perplexed parents who tell me that their baby was a fabulous sleeper from when he was tiny — slept well overnight and during the day — but at around six months something happened and that baby started to wake more overnight, sleep worse during the day and generally be a bit all over the place. It is very common for this change to happen around this age. Babies who were great sleepers can become poor sleepers and sometimes babies who were difficult sleepers all of a sudden start to sleep well.

If your baby's sleep gets worse around this age then the important thing is not to panic. I know that is easier said than done, but if you think about all these amazing things that are happening to your baby then you can understand why perhaps he is not sleeping so well. A lot of parents, because they are unsure of why their baby is waking, start to introduce things they hadn't previously been doing to get the baby to sleep. For example, they start to feed him overnight when they weren't previously, or they introduce other props such as rocking him to sleep, nursing him in their arms and having him sleep in their bed to overcome the sleep problem. This is a *big* no-no! An older baby really loves it when he doesn't have to do any work to get himself off to sleep, and so if you are doing that work or using a prop to get him off to sleep, he will grab onto that and go with it. You only have to use a new intervention a couple of times for a baby to think that he now *needs* that every time he goes to sleep and you will find yourself using it more and more until there is no other way your baby will go off to sleep.

So if this does happen, the way to deal with it is to *not* introduce anything new. Make sure he is getting plenty of kilojoules during the day and if you are just starting him on solids then you may want to introduce the second or third meal. Use the Babybliss Settling Technique to get him back to sleep overnight if he wakes when he is not due to, and if you maintain the routine you have been using then the waking should pass and he should return to being a good sleeper.

## CASE STUDY
### Charlie

When Charlie was eight weeks old he started to sleep for really long stints overnight. His parents were delighted and everyone was getting plenty of sleep. This went on until Charlie was about six months. At first he started waking just once overnight. Because he had only just started on solids, his parents thought he might be hungry and so they decided that if they fed him then it might pass after a day or two. This was not the case! Charlie loved the overnight feeding and one wake per night quickly became two then three and after a couple of weeks Charlie was now waking every two hours overnight. As you can imagine, his parents were completely beside themselves. They had had four months of great sleep and now they were up for a good part of the night.

When I spoke to his parents they told me that he was now on full solids and they were concerned about why he needed so much milk overnight. I explained that as babies get older they get more attached to sleep associations and they also like to take the path of least resistance. So if they are being helped to get back to sleep overnight, like with a breastfeed or a bottle, and they don't have to do it themselves, they will always take that option.

The way to get Charlie back to his sleeping best was to eliminate all the overnight feeding. At his age and weight — he weighed a healthy eight kilograms — and also the fact that he was on solids and hadn't been fed overnight for many months, meant that he could go all night without a feed. I told his parents that if they wanted to they could give him an early-morning feed, any time between 4.30 and 5.30 am, but they should first try to get him to go all night without feeding. They were to use the Babybliss Settling Technique to get him to go back to sleep and after a couple of nights he should be sleeping most if not all of the night himself. I also asked them to keep a record of what happened overnight so they, and I, could see that things were improving each night.

I explained that there would be one period overnight when Charlie could be awake for a very long time. Some babies who are really addicted to their prop can be awake for up to two hours, but if you can stick it out and not give in to them and give them what they were having previously, then that usually will be the worst it will be and after getting through the first night things can improve really quickly.

Charlie's mum reported that they had a really bad first night. Charlie was easy to settle prior to midnight but around midnight he woke and was awake for close to two hours. Charlie's mum nearly gave in and fed him, but she persevered and he finally went to sleep around 2 am. He then woke at 4.30 am and took about 30 minutes to go back to sleep, and then woke for the day at 6.30 am.

The second night was much better. There was no two-hour wake but Charlie did wake more frequently. I explained that this is normal. On the third night he woke briefly at 2 am and was very easy to settle. He slept through to 6.20 am.

After that, Charlie didn't require any help to get back to sleep. His parents heard him stir for the next couple of nights but he managed to get himself back to sleep. After the sixth night they didn't hear a peep out of him.

## Sleeping summary

Six months is a transitional age for a baby, so you can have sleep disturbances. It is really important not to introduce anything new to help get your baby to sleep, and try to teach him how to self-settle overnight and during the day if he is not doing that already.

Things to remember at this age:

+ Teach your baby to drop any sleep associations.
+ Resettle him overnight with the Babybliss Settling Technique.
+ His sleep cycles will get slightly longer at night and more like ours.
+ Drop down to one night feed — in the early morning.
+ Really get your routine happening.
+ Make sure your baby is having two good sleeps during the day, totalling about three to three-and-a-half hours.

# Baby feeding

You can start to introduce solids to a baby at around six months. This is an exciting time but can also be a stressful one if your baby is not really interested in eating and it is a struggle to get anything into her. The best way to manage this milestone is to let the baby set the pace on how fast to increase the amount of food she is taking.

Some parents start solids before six months and that is fine as long as you have sought advice from a health professional. However, the World Health Organization states that babies need only human milk or infant formula to grow and develop — that means no other food or fluids, including water — until they are six months of age.

It is worth knowing that introducing solids early does not necessarily help with such things as sleeping better overnight and/or symptoms of reflux, so unless you have been instructed by your GP or a health professional to start solids early, then I recommend holding off till around six months. At this time your baby may show signs that she is ready for solids. These signs include:

✦ interest in food eaten by you or others around her

✦ opens her mouth and is able to suck puréed food off a spoon

✦ wants to feed more often than she was previously

✦ she can sit while being supported, with good control of her head and neck.

You don't need to force solids on to your baby. If she is ready then she should be happy to open her mouth and try what you are offering. Remember, babies respond differently to different food types so don't be put off something if your baby rejects it the first time you offer it. A baby's palate is very immature and so you need to keep presenting and re-presenting different foods until she gets used to them. If she initially rejects something, wait a week or so and try it again.

There are loads of really good baby food books on the market and so if you can, grab yourself one of those, or borrow one, as they contain ideas on what foods you should offer first and great recipes for babies. Otherwise, ask an experienced friend or a relative what they did and how they introduced solids — often friends will have great tips and recipes for you too.

## How much should I feed and how much does she need?

### Breastfeeding

From about six to nine months a baby will continue to have about four to five breastfeeds in 24 hours. You may find that once your baby has started on solid foods, however, her interest in the milk might drop off. That is perfectly okay as long as she is eating well and gaining weight. If she is sleeping all night without an early morning feed, she can drop down to four feeds a day.

This can also be a frustrating time for breastfed babies, and their mums, as the feeds may become shorter but the baby might be increasingly distracted at feed time. It can be that she wants to move about more and really does not like being still for too long. If you are having trouble then try to feed her in a quiet area away from noise, TV and any other distractions. Obviously this won't be possible if you are out and about, but hopefully she will get enough milk to keep her going.

The milk feed can come before the food when you first introduce solids, except at the evening feed. However, at eight months start with the food first and then the milk, except if she is starting her day around 6 am, when she can have the breastfeed first and then breakfast an hour later.

## Bottle-feeding

Bottle-fed babies should definitely be having only four to five bottles per day now, and they should be having about 200 to 240 millilitres per feed. The same principle applies to bottle-fed babies as it does to breastfed babies in that they may start to reduce the amount of milk they are drinking once they are having three meals with solids per day.

Bottle-fed babies usually aren't as distracted when feeding as breastfed babies, but if your baby is finding it difficult to keep still long enough to drink her milk, then take her away from as many distractions as you can when feeding her.

## What about cow's milk?

Cow's milk can be used in the preparation of foods when a baby is older than six months but you should really be feeding a baby breast milk or formula until she is 12 months old and then introduce cow's milk for her to drink. Obviously breast milk is best, so if you can continue to breastfeed your baby then you can do this for as long as you like.

## Getting a baby to take the bottle

It is often around this age that some mothers like to wean their babies completely or just get them to take a bottle or two per day. If your baby has been taking a bottle regularly of either expressed breast milk (EBM) or formula, you should have no trouble increasing the amount of bottles she is having. But if your baby has never really had a bottle then it can be very difficult to get her to take one.

I see a lot of women who are at their wits' end because they are returning to work very soon and their baby flat out refuses to take the bottle. So if you are planning to wean your baby, either partially or completely, before she is 12 months old, then I recommend getting her used to taking a bottle way before six months of age. Start around eight weeks and offer her the bottle every other day, of EBM or formula, although EBM would be the better option. Around four or five months increase the frequency to offering the bottle every day, so that when you do decide to wean there will be no problem.

If you are having difficulty getting your baby to take the bottle or you have left it later than recommended, start to offer it every day. Try giving it to your baby in the morning when she is most hungry, or at the early morning feed, if she is still having it, around 5 am. That way she is still quite sleepy and hungry and should not put up too much of a fuss.

The other thing to try is to distract the baby while giving her the bottle, so you could try walking around the house or going outside while offering the bottle. Then try to get her to suck while she is distracted. Often if you can just get her to have one or two sucks she will get the hang of it. It is also a great idea to get someone other than the breastfeeding mum to do it. Your baby might be feeling confused about why you aren't feeding her in the usual way and so she refuses the bottle.

Offer the bottle every day, even if she does not take it. I recommend giving her about 30 minutes to try the bottle and if she has not taken it at the end of this time then you can give her the breast. Babies need repetition to learn something new, so if you present the bottle to her, at the same time every day, she will become familiar with it, and the taste, even if it is only a little taste every day, and eventually she will take it.

You can also try bypassing the bottle altogether and offering your baby a sippy cup. Many mothers do this and if your baby is on solids then this could be the way to go. However, most babies don't drink as much milk from a cup as they do from a bottle, so you need to be sure that they are getting enough milk and other food before trying a cup. If you are concerned that they still need quite a lot of milk then I would persevere with the bottle.

I had a client not so long ago who was completely panic-stricken as she was about to go back to work and the baby just flat out refused to take the bottle. He would open his mouth but cry and cry and not do any sucking whatsoever. I spent a couple of hours with them trying to get him to take the bottle but he wouldn't take it from me either. I showed her how to distract him when offering the bottle and recommended she just keep offering it every day.

About three days before she was due to go back to work she called me and was delighted to report that the day before, after about a week of offering the bottle and him protesting quite strongly, when she offered it to him he just opened his mouth and happily drank the whole thing, just as though he had been doing it every day! She couldn't believe it but was, of course, extremely happy and relieved.

## Getting into solid food

### First foods

The most common first food that is given to babies is rice cereal, but you can also start with any of the following:

+ puréed cooked apple or pear
+ steamed and pureed vegetables like pumpkin, carrot or potato
+ mashed avocado or banana.

Generally, when you are starting your baby on solids you don't have to give the meal at the same time every day, but I encourage you to work towards having a regular mealtime. In the early stages, if a day is missed here and there then that is fine because milk is the most important part of your baby's diet, so always give the milk feed first and then the solids. Once he is around eight or nine months, however, the food becomes the most important thing so food can come first, followed by milk.

Never think that adding rice cereal to the milk feed is a good idea if you are bottle-feeding. Your baby needs to learn the difference between eating and drinking.

Start with just a teaspoon or two of solids, but if your baby loves the food and it is going down with little fuss, increase the amount to a couple of tablespoons at a time. Don't be discouraged if the food comes back out. Babies are used to sucking and so it can take some time for them to adjust to the different way of eating.

Introduce a new food every two to three days. If you are concerned about allergies, then you may want to go a bit slower. When he is happily eating one meal a day, you can add the second meal. If after a couple of weeks he is going along just fine and loving his new food, then introduce the third meal.

You should feed a baby according to his appetite, and some babies are very hungry little things while others are not so fussed. So if, after you have offered him a couple of tablespoons and he still looks like he wants more, give him some more. I always recommend following up the main meal (lunch or dinner) of vegetables or cereal with a dessert, such as puréed fruit. But make sure he is getting most of his main meal before you give him the sweeter food.

A useful trick if your baby is not so fussed on a new vegetable is to add a little puréed apple or pear to the vegetable to sweeten it up. Then, after a couple of days, reduce the amount of fruit and increase the amount of vegetable in the mix. Keep reducing the fruit until he is just getting the plain vegetable.

Once on solids, continue the milk feeds until he is having three meals a day. Then you can drop the milk feeds to four each 24 hours. Leave some time between milk feeds and solids, that way he will be able to fit it all in. If you do offer him solids immediately after a milk feed, he won't be very interested in the food.

It doesn't really matter what time of the day you offer the first solids but it can be helpful if you do it in the afternoon. The food will help to distract him if he is getting a bit tired and cranky but it is also worthwhile knowing that a tired baby will usually refuse the solids or at least not be all that interested. So try to offer them when he is happy and alert.

### Introducing protein

I don't have any issue with introducing protein such as red meat, chicken and fish once a baby is on three meals per day and is happily eating a good variety of vegetables, fruit and cereal. If you have a baby who is particularly hungry and you feel as though you can't fill him up then protein can solve that. If you introduce protein around the six to eight month mark make sure it is puréed well, but at around nine months you can start to make it a thicker consistency. Your baby needs to learn to chew even if he doesn't have teeth as his gums are really strong, so it is a good idea to mash rather than purée when your baby gets to about eight or nine months.

### How much food and when to offer it?

When starting your baby on solids you should offer one meal, or taste, per day. This can be at any time during the day but most people offer it either in the morning or in the afternoon. I recommend starting in the afternoon around 5 pm.

At first you can offer a couple of teaspoons to see how your baby goes, but if she is opening her mouth and the food is going down easily then increase the amount the next time. It is reasonable to feed a baby according to her appetite, so if you have a hungry baby who is just loving the new food, don't hold back. Give her what she wants and introduce the second and third meals over the course of the next week or two.

If your baby is not so interested in eating solids then go slowly and just keep offering one meal or two small meals for a couple of weeks or so. Let your baby set the pace and don't force food on her. She will accept it in her own time.

### Reactions to foods

Babies have a very strong gag reflex and often when you present a new food or a new texture of food they will gag. This is a normal reaction so don't be worried. But obviously you should be offering foods that are the appropriate texture for her age. When she is just starting on solids the food needs to be puréed and sloppy with no or very few small lumps. After a month or two of happily eating these foods you could then start to mash the food rather than purée it so it has a thicker consistency.

I believe that all food should be served warm as it does make a difference to the taste and I wouldn't want to eat my cooked vegetables cold. Obviously things like fruit and yoghurt are cold foods and so it is fine to offer them to your baby without heating. It can be difficult to know if your baby has had a reaction to a certain food, especially if you are mixing a couple of different foods together. Some babies will get a slight rash or red cheeks when you introduce a new food and this is usually okay.

The things to look out for if your baby has a bad reaction are:
+ projectile vomiting or vomiting large amounts
+ sudden onset of diarrhoea
+ hives
+ swelling or redness around her mouth soon after she has eaten
+ a mottled rash all over her body.

## Foods to avoid

There are some foods to avoid giving a baby until she is older:
+ Nuts are a choking hazard and peanuts can cause a severe allergic reaction in children so avoid all nuts until your baby is at least two years old.

- Raw or undercooked pieces of fruit and vegetables are also choking hazards.
- Honey can contain bacteria so it is best avoided until 12 months.
- Small hard food like popcorn or bread with seeds in it are a choking hazard.
- Strawberries can cause a bad reaction so it is best to wait till 12 months before offering.
- Egg yolks can be given at six months but egg whites should be avoided until after nine months.

## What if my baby refuses to eat?

If you find your baby has been eating well and then suddenly stops and refuses to open her mouth, don't panic. Just give her a break for a day or two and then offer the solids again. If you offer something new and she doesn't seem to like it, then wait a week before offering that food again. Keep presenting food regularly until your baby gets used to it. And I promise she will get used to it. Obviously we all have our likes and dislikes and we need to respect those dislikes, but a baby's palate is really immature so different flavours and textures may be rejected initially. Once she has tasted that flavour or texture a few times, however, she should be more used to it and happy to eat it.

## Will my baby get constipated?

Babies can get a bout of constipation when they start on solids but some parents do get a bit confused about what constipation actually is. If a baby is pooing every couple of days but when she does poo it is soft and pasty and she doesn't seem to be distressed by pooing, then she isn't constipated. However, if her poo is hard and looks like a rock or a pebble, then she could be constipated. There are a few things you can do to help relieve the constipation:

✦ avoid rice cereal and offer puréed fruit instead

✦ avoid bananas as they can be constipating

✦ offer her diluted prune juice in a bottle — make it up like you would cordial, with added boiled water

✦ offer water regularly with her meals, as increasing fluids can help with constipation.

## Other food problems

Some babies can eat too much at first as they are so excited about eating real food. This is uncommon as most babies will stop eating when they are full. But if your baby keeps opening her mouth and won't really stop eating and then vomits after the feed or is really hard to settle, you might want to limit the amount of food you are giving her.

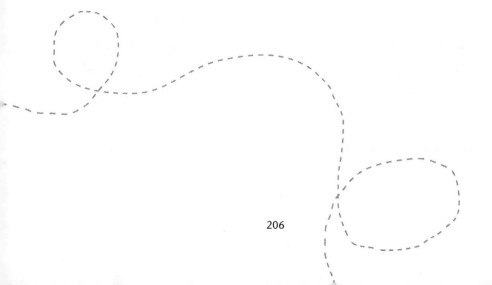

# Development and stimulation

Between six and nine months loads of wonderful things are happening to your baby both physically and emotionally. She is becoming a little individual aware that she is a separate person to you. She is more mobile, much more active and playful, looking, touching and exploring the world around her. This is also the age when babies can become a bit clingy with their mums, in particular, and have a bit of separation anxiety if Mum is not close by all the time.

Emotionally she will start to be able to separate her feelings and understand the difference between hunger, tiredness and fear, and so be able to let you know what it is she needs to deal with her feelings, like a snack or a cuddle.

She will also start to express her wants. She will point at things that she wants and display her distress when she doesn't get what she wants, or if you take something from her that she really, really wants. By nine months she will be very aware of who the important people in her life are and so be more sensitive and shy with strangers or people she is not so familiar with.

Physically between six and nine months a baby will be able to roll from her front on to her back and from her back on to her front. She will also be able to sit up unsupported and when she is on her tummy she will look like she is doing push-ups, pushing her chest up off the floor. She may also be able to move herself around the floor by some version of crawling, whether it be a commando style, a slide along on her bottom while sitting up, or a backwards slide, or the traditional, on all fours, crawl. She will also now be adept at grabbing and holding toys with both hands and will have found her feet, usually by grabbing them and putting them in her mouth when she is lying on her back.

During these months all those wonderful sounds she has been making will start to resemble actual words. She will also be able to do different things with her mouth like blow raspberries or make clicking noises and she will be able to mimic words that you say to her over and over. She may also start to say 'ma, ma, ma' or 'da, da, da' — you can decide between yourselves which one came first!

## Developmental milestones

At this age your baby will:

+ pass small items from one hand to the other
+ pick up an object using her thumb and finger
+ roll over on to her tummy and back again
+ sit up on her own (around eight months)

- ✦ start to move by pulling herself along on her tummy
- ✦ hold a bottle or a cup on her own
- ✦ reach out for objects and pick them up
- ✦ inspect things she picks up and feel with her hands before putting them in her mouth
- ✦ look towards loud sounds
- ✦ start to babble and can say 'da da' or 'ma ma'
- ✦ look towards the person when asked where they are — for example, 'Where is Daddy?'
- ✦ copy sounds made by others.

# Playing with your baby

This is a great age because your baby will be doing so many more things and be able to play with you and interact much more. Some things you can do to entertain and stimulate your baby are:

- ✦ talk to her and have her talk back
- ✦ point out her different body parts, such as her nose and play 'Where is your nose?'
- ✦ play with toys that she can put things in to or take things out of
- ✦ play music and get her to bang on an 'instrument'
- ✦ take her outside and point out all the wonderful things to look at.

A baby of this age can become bored quite easily if you don't stimulate her, but that doesn't mean you have to sit with her or have her on your hip all the time. You need to teach your baby how to play happily on her own as well as with others, and so I encourage you to let your baby play on her own so she can learn to be happy playing and entertaining herself and not always be looking for someone to be with her. A lot of babies at this age can be a bit clingy with their mother and are unhappy to be left to play on their own. It is a good idea to let her play on the floor without actually sitting with her, and if she does protest then let her know where you are and stay in sight. If she really doesn't want to be left alone then you can sit with her but let her play on her own. After a day or two, start to move away from her for short periods of time always coming back when she starts to protest.

If you leave the room then tell her where you are going and, when you come back, make sure she knows you are back in the room. You can make a ritual of leaving the room, so every time you leave say the same thing to her and when you come back say the same thing. Eventually, although she might not understand the words, she will become familiar with the ritual and not be too upset when you walk away from her.

# Chapter 9

# Your independent baby: nine to 12 months

# Baby sleeping

Between nine and 12 months you should have your baby in a really great little routine with his sleeping. He should be having two sleeps during the day, totalling about two-and-a-half to three hours and be sleeping all night — 11 to 12 hours. If he is still having that early morning feed but he is eating well during the day, then now is probably the time for you to drop that extra feed and get him sleeping through till morning.

It can be tricky to get a baby who is used to waking around 5 am to sleep through to somewhere after 6 am as he will come out of his dream sleep around 5 am and can be quite wakeful. But he should go back into a deep sleep — the second-deepest sleep of the night — around 5 am and so if you consistently settle him back to sleep for a couple of days he will start to sleep through that waking time.

Now when I say 'resettle' I mean by using the Babybliss Settling Technique, and you need to do it until he goes back to sleep. The first time you do it, because he will be quite wakeful, it might take some time for him to settle — up to about 45 minutes or so — but the important thing is to stick with it till he does go back to sleep. Don't just give up, as that way he won't learn that he can go back to sleep and get some really good, deep sleep.

## When should my baby sleep and for how long?

At nine months a baby can be awake for about three hours at a time but usually a baby really can't last as long in the morning as he can during the rest of the day, so he may only be able to stay awake for about two-and-a-half hours at that time. By 12 months your baby should be able to stay awake for up to four hours at a time, but again, he might be more tired in the morning and ready to have his morning nap around 9 to 9.30 am.

He will still be having two lovely sleeps during the day and, if it hasn't already happened, then around ten or 11 months I recommend reducing the first sleep to about 45 minutes only. You still want him to be having about one-and-a-half to two hours in the afternoon, and to manage that you need to reduce the amount of sleep he is getting in the morning. If you do need to wake him up, make it a gentle wake, either by just opening the door or opening the curtains and if you have to, giving him a gentle rub on the back and then letting him wake up naturally.

He should be going to bed at around 7 pm and sleeping 11 to 12 hours overnight with no night feeding. So in summary:

| Age | Up-time | Down-time | Average sleeps |
| --- | --- | --- | --- |
| 9 months | 2½ to 3 hours | 1½ to 2 hours | Two definite day sleeps totalling about 3 hours, and 11 to 12 hours per night. |
| 12 months | 3½ to 4 hours | 45 minutes in the morning and 1½ to 2 hours in the afternoon. | Two day sleeps totalling about 2 to 2½ hours, and 11 to 12 hours overnight. |

## Babybliss routine and ritual

By now you will know that babies love routine and ritual and you really should have an established routine happening by now. At this age babies have developed expectation and so they can understand that the day has a pattern and that one thing follows another. I believe that because of this babies who have a good routine feel very secure and are confident little people. They know what the day will hold and, with the familiar rituals prior to events like sleeping and feeding, they are not surprised by any of those things occurring and usually won't be so resistant because they are prepared.

Having a ritual around leaving or separating from your baby too, means that you will have a child who won't be distressed if you walk away from him or leave him with someone else. Try to repeat the same thing every time you leave and every time you come back, even if you are just going into another room of your house.

A good routine for a baby of this age would be as follows:

| | |
|---|---|
| 6 to 6.30 am | Up for the day. Wait about 15 minutes or so before offering the breast or bottle-feed. |
| 7 to 7.30 am | Breakfast. (Note: If your baby wakes around 7 am then he can have his breakfast first and his milk feed about 8 to 8.30 am.) |
| 9 to 9.30 am | Morning sleep. It is a good idea to have a regular time that your baby goes down for her naps. This needs to be the same every day, give or take 30 minutes. |
| 10.30 am | Morning tea snack. (Note: This is optional, if your baby is asleep or not interested, don't worry. It is useful, though, to distract her if she is looking for a milk feed.) |
| 11.30 to 12 pm | Lunchtime. |

| | |
|---|---|
| 12.45 to 1 pm | Breastfeed or bottle-feed. This can be replaced with a sippy cup if you are bottle-feeding. |
| 1.30 pm | Afternoon sleep. This sleep should be about 1½ to 2 hours. |
| 3.30 to 4 pm | Afternoon tea snack — the same as morning tea. |
| 5 to 5.30 pm | Dinner. |
| 6 pm | Bathtime, then a quiet playtime. |
| 6.30 pm | Breastfeed or bottle-feed. |
| 7 pm | Bedtime. Bedtime ritual must always be the same. |

## Sleeping problems

### I can't get my baby to sleep past 5 am!

Most babies need to sleep past 5 am. They can be a bit wakeful at this time because they have just had about five hours of dream sleep and light non-dream sleep but they are geared to drop back into some lovely deep sleep from about 5 am so they need to be encouraged to have this sleep. If your baby is waking early, don't get her up and start the day. If you do get her up early then she will not learn to sleep later and will actually be quite tired until she is put back down for her morning nap. That is because she has missed out on the last bit of her night sleep.

Another way of encouraging this unwanted early-morning wake is by putting your baby back down for her morning nap too early in the day. And often we do this because the baby is tired and grizzly and looks like she needs a sleep. But she is tired and grizzly because she has not finished her night sleep. So what happens is she gets to finish off her night sleep at her morning nap, which is usually a fairly long, deep sleep. Essentially, her night sleep becomes separated. The way to teach her to sleep longer is by keeping her up until around 9 am, no matter what time she has started the day, and then letting her have her morning nap. Then when she wakes early the following morning, use the settling technique to get her back to sleep and make sure you keep doing it until she has gone to sleep — that is important. And again, put her down for her morning nap at around 9 am. Keep up this routine until she is sleeping past 5 am.

There are babies who are genuine early morning wakers, but these are few and far between. I always encourage parents to use all the tricks and techniques to get a baby to sleep later before allocating them to the Early Risers Club. I find that it is usually boys who are the natural early risers rather than girls, but there is always an exception to that rule.

If you have tried resetting at 5 am and keeping her up later in the morning and you are still not having any success, you could try putting your baby down to sleep 60 minutes later than you normally would at night and then resettle in the morning as well as keeping her morning nap time at 9 am. This is what I like to call the 'Triple Treat'. It will mean that you will have to employ all your distraction methods to get her to stay awake for an extra hour but because she is missing out on that one sleep cycle at the beginning of the night she should be easier to resettle at 5 am or, even better, sleep right past it.

When you have got her sleeping till a reasonable time — that is, any time after 6 am — and she has been doing it for about two to three weeks, you can start to bring her bedtime back to around 7 pm. Every couple of days, put her to bed 15 minutes earlier than you had been. For example, if you were putting her down at 8 pm, put her down at 7.45 pm instead. After three days of this, put her down for the night at 7.30 pm, and keep moving the time back every three days until you are back to 7 pm, which is the ideal time for a young child to go to bed.

## CASE STUDY
### Edward

Edward was a great sleeper during the day and night but he had a habit of waking up to start the day at 4.30 am. Not good! Sometimes he would get to 5 am, but most of the time it was around 4.30 am. Edward was 11 months old. His parents felt they had tried everything to get Edward to sleep longer in the morning but nothing seemed to work.

I asked them what was happening with his day sleeps and his mum told me that because he was getting up so early he was exhausted by about 7.30 am and so they were putting him down to sleep then. He would usually have a good morning nap and then a shorter afternoon nap. They were also putting him down at around 8 pm in an attempt to get him to sleep later in the morning. It wasn't working.

Babies need to be asleep by around 7 pm. That way, they get a good four to five hours of deep sleep before they transition into their dream sleep around midnight. If they have all this deep sleep, it usually then sets them up to have a good night's sleep and also means they sleep in later in the morning. So putting a baby down later in the evening in order to get them to sleep longer just does not work.

I asked Edward's parents to make sure to put him to bed around 7 pm and then, when he woke early in the morning, they were to use the Babybliss Settling Technique to get him back to sleep. Even if he didn't go back to sleep, he was to stay in his cot till at least 6 am and then he was to have his morning nap at 9 am, not earlier.

They did this for three days and then called to let me know that although he was still waking early, it was 5.30 am when he woke and they were able to keep him in his cot till at least 6.15 am. His morning nap was happening at 9 am and he was sleeping for 60 minutes and his afternoon nap had now increased to 90 minutes.

After another three days they reported very happily that Edward had started to sleep in till 6 am and occasionally 6.15

am. He was having good sleeps during the day and going to bed at 7 pm every night. A much better pattern all round.

## Sleeping summary

Things to remember in terms of sleep for this age are:

✦ Make sure your routine is happening the same way every day.

✦ Put your baby to bed around 7 pm every night.

✦ Your baby should be having two day sleeps, totalling about two-and-a-half to three hours.

✦ Your baby should be sleeping all night, so drop the early-morning feed if it is still happening.

✦ The first sleep of the day can be shortened but the second sleep should be at least 90 minutes.

✦ If your baby is waking before 6 am then you need to work on him sleeping later.

✦ Be consistent.

# Baby feeding

By the time a baby is nine months she should be well and truly into her solids. She should be eating three solid meals a day — breakfast, lunch and dinner — and having morning and afternoon tea snacks if she wants them. At nine months she will also drop down to about three milk feeds per day and that will continue on till she is around 12 months old.

It is around this age that you may find your baby wants to be more involved in the feeding process, and although that can be a bit frustrating for you, it is a great developmental stage for her, to want to feed herself. As well as feeding her mashed food you can now start to offer her finger food — that is, food she can pick up and put in her mouth with little or no assistance from you and which is ideal for her to feed herself.

You may also notice that dinnertime (and lunchtime and breakfast) is becoming very messy, with her and the floor getting covered in food. This also is very normal. Babies love to play and so eating can become a game for them too. The 'throwing everything I have on the floor so Mummy can pick it up and we can start all over again' game is a very common, yet very frustrating game that most babies will play. While it can be okay to let your baby do this — and quite frankly it is pretty hard to stop it —you need to ensure she is aware that she does need to eat some food. So while she is trying to feed herself the finger food, you can also be feeding her the mushy stuff from a spoon. That way she will get enough food but still learn how to feed herself.

It is a good idea to have a set time for eating, and that the mealtime isn't too long. Thirty minutes is probably plenty of time to get enough food into her little tummy, and if mealtimes go on for too long she will get bored, start to complain and refuse to do what you want. Also, don't ever force-feed your baby. I know it is incredibly frustrating when you have spent a lot of the day preparing wonderful combinations of mushy vegetables and then she won't open her mouth to try the food, but you don't want to make mealtimes a negative or teary time for her. She needs to enjoy her meals with little or no fuss and the last thing you want as her parent is for her to have an unhealthy attitude towards eating. If she doesn't like a particular thing then give it a break for a while and try it again at a later date. Don't fight with her over food. She is too young to understand the consequences of not eating her lunch. Just make sure she gets enough of what she does like, and perhaps a couple of spoonfuls of something new.

I also believe that it is really important to expand a baby's taste, so once she has been eating well for a while don't be afraid to experiment with flavours and choices. A baby who is introduced early to lots of different flavours, tastes and textures usually becomes a great little eater and will try anything, within reason of course. Between nine and 12 months the food you offer can be more lumpy in consistency and cooked food can be mashed rather than puréed.

Eating with your baby is nice for you too, especially when you are trying out a new food. If you sit down and show her that you are eating the same food then she might be less reluctant to give it a go. You can also let her take the food from your plate, as most babies will want to eat what you are having — for some reason it looks more appetising.

## How much should I feed and how much does he need?

At this age you can let your baby set the pace as to how much food he wants but as a general guideline he should be having about three milk feeds a day. Some breastfed babies might still be having a breastfeed around 3 or 4 pm, however, and that is okay, although I recommend dropping that afternoon feed by the time he is 12 months old.

Continue to increase the amount of solids you are offering him as he is finishing off each amount. So if you find that at around 10 months your baby is finishing everything you are offering him, then increase each serving size. At this age your baby should be eating about a cup of food at every meal, with some dessert offered at lunch and dinner. He should also be having a snack at morning and afternoon teatime.

You may find that at certain meals he eats more, which is absolutely normal. Offer breakfast first if he is sleeping till after

6.30 am and then he can have his milk after that, before he goes back for his morning sleep.

Your baby should be steadily gaining weight and you should notice that he is filling out a bit more now that he has been on solids for a couple of months. But, of course, you should still get him weighed intermittently to check on his weight gain. If you are concerned about his weight then weigh him more frequently.

## Using a sippy cup

By now you may have started offering your baby cool boiled water in a 'sippy' cup. This is the term I use for all those wonderful spill-proof cups that are available. It is a good idea to offer your baby water in a cup rather than a bottle, as a lot of breastfed babies won't take a bottle anyway. By offering him the cup he will get the hang of using it sooner rather than later.

He can have water at mealtimes and it is also absolutely fine to offer it throughout the day as well, when he is not due for a milk feed. Be aware that your baby may be thirsty, especially during the summer months, so it is good to have a cup of water on the go all the time.

# Development and stimulation

Between nine and 12 months things take on a different pace, usually a much faster pace. Your baby will now be moving around and exploring her world with great excitement and vigour. Parents usually say this is the most fun time with a baby as she is much more playful, chatty and loves being around people, and her personality really begins to show. You can also be more mobile, being able to take her out for longer periods during the day, and she will enjoy her outings much more.

If your baby has displayed any separation anxiety in the previous months, it should start to decrease in these three months. She can now start to understand that when you go away you will return and so she doesn't need to be frightened about that any more.

Babies become much more independent in their likes and dislikes in these months and she will have no trouble letting you know that she is not happy getting dressed or that she wants to be off the change table and on the floor. She can do this by kicking her legs, rolling over to get away from what you are doing and verbally letting you know by yelling or whingeing.

The biggest change that happens in these three months is her mobility. Your baby will be able to move herself around much more efficiently. She will either be crawling — in whatever manner suits her — and she should also start to pull herself up to stand on her feet. She will do this by hanging onto the furniture or onto you, and once she has mastered this skill she will want to do it all the time. There will be no more quiet play sitting in one spot: she will now want to move around the house and try to use and perfect her new skill. Some babies may start to walk during this time, which is a very exciting milestone. But don't be worried if your baby hasn't started to walk by 12 months. She will get there eventually.

Babies now can begin to have more recognisable 'conversations'. Although you might not understand the words she is using, she will definitely be babbling on more and sounding like she is talking to you. You may recognise some words, like 'Ma ma ma' or 'Da da', and she may point at objects and say what almost sounds like the word, like 'light' or 'bird' or 'shoe'. She will also start to shake her head when she means 'no', and this can be somewhat frustrating as she may like to do it all the time, especially at mealtimes.

She will become more interested in playing with toys and start to examine objects rather than just put them in her mouth. She will also look towards sounds much more and seem to understand you and what you are saying.

# Developmental milestones

At this age your baby should:

✦ know her name and turn her head when her name is called

✦ be more aware of strangers and not be so happy to go to them

✦ be able to give you lovely cuddles

✦ be unhappy when Mummy (or her main care-giver) leaves her sight

✦ hold her arms out to be picked up

✦ babble a lot and like to be talked to

✦ love to be played with

✦ copy certain gestures like shaking her head, waving and coughing

✦ be pointing at things

✦ shake and nod her head to indicate 'no' and 'yes'

✦ love to look at books and pictures and point out certain objects when asked.

## Playing with your baby

This is a great age for playing with your baby as he will really love it and he can get involved in certain games. Make sure you let your baby play on his own from time to time and learn to reach and move towards the things he wants. Some things you can do to entertain and stimulate your baby are:

+ play music and songs — he will love to rock or bounce to the music
+ give him toys that he can open and shut or put things in or through
+ read simple books to him while pointing out objects in the illustrations and repeating the names or sounds they make — for example, 'a cat says meow'
+ give him a trolley to push
+ give him a musical instrument, like a wooden spoon to bang on a saucepan.

## Going back to work: childcare options

It can be around this age that the full-time carer, be it Mum or Dad, may need to return to work so you will have to decide on what sort of childcare you will use. If you intend to put your baby in childcare then it is a good option to plan ahead. As everyone is aware, childcare places are limited, especially in city areas, so start to scout around for a centre in your area at least six months before you intend to go back to work.

Also consider what type of childcare facility you would like your baby to be in — either a large centre or a smaller one, family day-care or having a nanny come to your home. Discuss the options with your partner and whoever else has a care-giver role in your baby's life and do the research. You don't want to leave the decision to the last minute and then have to take whatever option is offered to you. You need to be in control of this.

## What are the options?

These days childcare is a much talked about issue, with limited spaces available in childcare centres and also debate about what options are best for young children. Obviously all your options depend on your situation, both financial and social, so it is difficult for me to advise what I think is the best idea as I don't want anyone to feel uncomfortable about having to use an option that they really have no choice about.

That said, I will say that one-on-one care is the ideal option for a young child, and by that I mean a baby under about 12 months. By one-on-one care I mean that the baby is looked after solely by one person, be it a nanny, a relative or a friend. If that is not an option for you, then the next best thing is a centre or a family day-care that has a good ratio of carers to babies. Ideally, the ratio should be something like one carer to three young babies.

If you have decided to use a larger childcare centre, then do all the work beforehand and get all the statistics and information you can about the place.

The things to ask and look out for in a childcare centre include:

✦ What is the carer-to-baby ratio?
✦ Does the centre have appropriate safety features, like child-proof gates, fences and sun protection outside?

+ Do they put sunscreen on the children if they go outside?
+ Do they insist the children wear hats when playing outside?
+ If they provide meals what types of food are served?
+ Is there a process for signing the child in and out?
+ Is there an incident-reporting process?
+ Is the centre clean?
+ Do the carers have appropriate qualifications?
+ Can you get testimonials from other parents?

The things to look for when employing a nanny include:

+ What are their qualifications?
+ Do they have experience working with young babies?
+ Do they have a driver's licence with no fines or disqualifications?
+ Have you done a working-with-children check and a police check?
+ What is their background and have they spent a lot of time around families and children?
+ Do they know how to play and entertain a child of your baby's age?

## How to maintain the Babybliss routine

It is perfectly reasonable to ask the staff at your childcare centre to stick to your routine as much as they possibly can, and most of them will be compliant and happy to do what they can. You may need to take into consideration the travel time and so on, and adjust the times of the day sleeps but try to match them as closely as possible to what is happening at home.

It can be a bit tricky getting a baby to go off to sleep on his own in an open-plan environment with lots of other children around, but your baby should adjust so long as the carers are not patting him off to sleep every time, or rocking him in their arms, or doing any of those things that you have worked so hard to eliminate. If they need to settle him in and get him sleeping well they can use the Babybliss Settling Technique to help him get used to the unfamiliar environment and sleeping well. You should also talk the carers through the pre-sleep rituals you use so they will do the same thing. Also, if your baby has a comforter or a special toy he sleeps with, you should make sure that it goes with him to the centre. If he is sleeping in a sleeping bag, then make sure he is put into that at every sleep time.

It is important for your baby to have the same routine at the centre as he is having at home. Going to childcare is a big thing for a little person, and a big change for him to be away from his home and away from you. But if you can maintain as much familiarity as possible for him then the transition should not be too hard.

# Chapter 10

# Welcome to the toddler world: 12 to 18 months

# Baby sleeping

Congratulations! You have made it through the first year of your baby's life — and lived to tell the tale. Hopefully it's been an amazing experience so far, with the few hiccups along the way managed brilliantly by you. You now have an energetic toddler on your hands and life will have stepped up a notch. Toddlers are designed to keep you on your toes. They are little explorers, trying to find out everything they can about the world around them. Their growth and development at this time can be astounding, and frightening to both you and to them.

## When should my baby sleep and for how long?

Hopefully you will have a toddler who is now a great sleeper. From 12 months of age your toddler should be routinely sleeping 11 to 12 hours per night, be able to stay awake for four to five hours during the day and be reducing his two daytime sleeps down to one per day. This should be done by the time he is around 16 months of age. His daytime naps should total about two to three hours and overnight he should be sleeping through with no feeding at all. While he is still having his morning nap, it should be around 9 to 9.30 am, as babies are usually ready to go back to bed at that time of the day. His afternoon nap should be around 1.30 pm, but once you have dropped the morning sleep then this can move back to around 12 to 12.30 pm. So in summary:

| Age | Up-time | Down-time | Average sleeps |
| --- | --- | --- | --- |
| 12 months | 3½ to 4 hours | 45 minutes in the morning, and 1½ to 2 hours in the afternoon. | Two day sleeps totalling 2 to 2½ hours, and 11 to 12 hours overnight. |
| 18 months | 4 to 5 hours | One sleep around lunchtime for 2 to 3 hours. | One sleep per day, and 11 to 12 hours overnight. |

## When should I drop the day sleeps down to one?

Dropping down to one sleep can take some time, and you need to let your toddler set the pace at which this is done. Some toddlers need two daytime sleeps until they are around 16 months old, while others can drop down to one sleep around 12 months without too much trouble.

I recommend that at around 11 to 12 months of age, if you haven't already, start to reduce the length of your baby's morning nap. So if he is having 90 minutes, then cut it down to 45 to 60 minutes. If he is only having 60 minutes, then cut it down to

30 to 45 minutes. This is the sleep that he will eventually drop, so you want to keep reducing the need for it. The second sleep of the day is the most important sleep as it is the one that he will keep so ensure that he is still getting at least 90 minutes at this time of the day.

When you start reducing the morning sleep, that doesn't mean you have to bring the second sleep forward in the day. You need to keep putting him down at the same time you were previously. For example, if he was sleeping from 9 to 10.30 am and then 1.30 to 3 pm, he will now be sleeping from 9 to 9.45 am, and then 1.30 to 3 pm.

Keep him on this schedule till you find that when you put him down for his morning nap he won't go to sleep or you have had a few days where he has skipped his morning nap without too much trouble. Another sign that he is ready to move to one sleep is if he happily has his morning sleep but is very difficult to get to sleep in the afternoon. Once you do drop the morning nap you may need to then bring the afternoon sleep back in the day, so he is going down around 12 or 12.30 pm. He will keep this day sleep for as long as he needs it. Some children still have a daytime sleep until they go off to school at five years of age, so don't push him to give it up if you feel he still needs it. Also, toddlers are so energetic and active that they really do need to have that sleep in the middle of the day. The nap will give him energy for the afternoon and it also means that you won't have a screaming wreck of a child on your hands by 5 pm.

There are some babies who continue to have a longer morning sleep than afternoon sleep. If you are unable to work it so that he has a shorter morning nap and a longer afternoon nap, you can start to move the morning nap closer to midday. For example, you would slowly move the morning nap from 9.30 am to around 11 am, and let him have a short afternoon nap around 3 pm. After a while, if you feel he is coping and not really needing that afternoon sleep, start putting him down for one sleep around midday.

## Babybliss routine and ritual

This is a transitional age for most babies and they are now old enough to work towards dropping down from two day sleeps to one day sleep. This can occur any time from about 12 months to 18 months. Because of that, I have included a routine for when your baby is still having two sleeps per day and then when they move to one sleep.

### *Babybliss routine with two day sleeps*

| | |
|---|---|
| 6 to 6.30 am | Up for the day. |
| 7 to 7.30 am | Breakfast followed by a milk feed, either breast or bottle/cup. |
| 9 to 9.30 am | Morning sleep. This sleep should be no longer than 45 minutes. |
| 10.30 am | Morning tea snack. |
| 11.30 am to 12 pm | Lunchtime. |

| 12.45 to 1 pm | Milk feed, either breast or bottle/cup. |
| 1.30 pm | Afternoon sleep. This sleep should be about 1½ to 2 hours. |
| 3.30 to 4 pm | Afternoon tea snack. |
| 5 to 5.30 pm | Dinnertime. |
| 6 pm | Bathtime, then a quiet playtime. |
| 6.30 pm | Breastfeed or bottle-feed. |
| 7 pm | Bedtime. Bedtime ritual must always be the same. |

## Babybliss routine with one day sleep

| 6 to 6.30 am | Up for the day. |
| 7 to 7.30 am | Breakfast followed by a milk feed either breast or bottle/cup. |
| 9.30 to 10 am | Morning tea snack. |
| 11.30 am | Lunchtime. |
| 12 to 12.30 pm | Daytime sleep. This sleep should be about 2 to 3 hours. |
| 3.30 to 4 pm | Afternoon tea snack. |

| | |
|---|---|
| 5 to 5.30 pm | Dinnertime. |
| 6 pm | Bathtime, then a quiet playtime. |
| 6.30 pm | Breast, bottle (or cup) feed. |
| 7 pm | Bedtime. Bedtime ritual must always be the same. |

## Sleeping problems

The common sleeping problems that occur around this time are babies who won't sleep well during the day, which usually means they need to move to one sleep a day, and babies who wake early in the morning, before 6 am. If this is happening with your baby then please read the previous chapter, where I discussed early morning wakes and how to get past them (pages 216–220).

Your baby should be sleeping through the night too, so if that is not happening then read pages 156–164, where I discussed how to get rid of sleep associations. You can also read up on the Babybliss Settling Technique (pages 143–145) to use when teaching your baby to sleep all night.

Another common problem that can arise as your baby gets older is that he starts to require you to be with him when he goes off to sleep. An older baby, usually over ten months of age, can often like someone staying with him until he goes off to sleep, and he will keep checking that you remain close by. If you happen to leave the room before he is asleep he will protest by standing up and yelling out for you to come back. Once you have returned he will calm down and attempt to go off to sleep, but only if you remain in the room. Often you don't even have to be touching him, he just really wants to know you are near him.

At this age you should be a bit firmer with your settling and obviously you need to be out of the room when he finally goes off to sleep. By that I mean you can stay with your baby and use the Babybliss Settling Technique to get him to calm down, but you need to then leave the room when he is calm but not asleep. If he then protests by yelling or crying, you should wait between three and five minutes before going back in to his room. Never let your baby cry for more than five minutes, but at this age you should give him the opportunity to calm himself down and go off to sleep, and that time seems to be long enough for him to do that. If after that time he is still crying go back in and stay with him until he is calm. No matter how long it takes, you need to leave the room as soon as he is calm and, again, wait between three and five minutes.

You need to keep doing this until he goes off to sleep and the first time you do it, it might take a while. But if you are out of the room when he finally does go to sleep, he will learn that he does not actually need you to be there. After a couple of days of doing this you will find that he should happily go off to sleep without your having to go back in to settle him.

# CASE STUDY
## Estella

Estella was around 16 months when I first met her and her parents. She was a great sleeper overnight and during the day once she went to sleep, but it was the getting to sleep that was the problem. It could take her parents anywhere from 20 minutes to two hours to get her off to sleep and the longer it went on the longer it was taking.

Estella would stand up and cry once she had been put down and her parents had to sit beside her cot until she went to sleep. They didn't have to touch her but if they went to leave the room she was up on her feet, clutching onto the side of the cot and screaming. So ultimately they sat with her until she went to sleep, which often took hours.

When I visited them I explained how older babies become very attached to someone being in the room with them while they go off to sleep, and so what we were going to do that night was put Estella to bed after the night-time ritual and then we were going to leave the room for five minutes. We did that and she immediately stood up as Mum turned to leave. We let her protest for the full five minutes and then Mum went back in and lay her down. She stayed with Estella, rubbing her back until she was calm, which took about two minutes, and then she left the room again.

Estella's mum repeated this process four times, each repetition it was taking less time for Estella to calm down. After the fourth time, Estella didn't protest at all when her mum left the room. She did make a couple of whingeing, sleepy sounds but after a few minutes there was silence. This process took a total of 25 minutes and after another ten minutes of silence I popped my head in to see what was happening and Estella was sound asleep.

Estella's parents could not quite believe it as she hadn't fallen asleep that quickly in a very long time. The second night was even better, with her mum only returning to Estella's room three times to lie her down and calm her, and on the third night they didn't have to go back in to her room at all.

## Sleeping summary

Things to remember in terms of sleep for this age are:

+ Watch out for signs that your baby may need to drop to one sleep a day.
+ Teach your baby to sleep till at least 6 am if she is not already doing it.
+ Routine and ritual needs to be maintained and used by all your baby's carers.
+ Older babies get very attached to someone being in the room when they go off to sleep so try to make sure you are out of the room when your baby finally goes to sleep.

# Baby feeding

Feeding a toddler can be a frustrating experience that can push you to your limits. At times you might feel like you are fighting a losing battle, but take heart, you are not alone. Most toddlers around this age become fussier about eating and can flat out refuse to eat anything you give them.

The best way to get through these trying times is to remember that you are the boss but also remember not to make too much of a fuss of mealtimes. You don't want your toddler to hate sitting down for a meal, so you need to let go of your frustration and not fight about food. It is at this age that your toddler will want to be in control of her eating, which means she will want to feed herself much more and also she will only want to eat what she thinks she likes. You may need to be a bit creative to get the food she needs into her.

Finger food is what most toddlers want to eat, so offer her plenty of options of fruit and vegetables that she can pick up and feed herself. It is also a good idea to have a variety of different food options, and not give her the same thing every night for dinner because you know that is what she will eat. Children learn through repetition, so if you offer your toddler a different food and she takes a bite of it, eventually she will come to expect that food will be offered and she will start to eat it. If you offer her only things you know she likes and not alternatives, you will find in the years ahead that you have a child who won't eat or even try anything new.

## How much should I feed and how much does she need?

Toddlers often eat on the go, which means you might have to offer her regular snacks during the day to fill her up as she doesn't usually like sitting in the highchair for too long. That doesn't mean you should forgo having her sit in her chair or at the table for mealtimes as young children need to be taught that mealtimes are important and are when you all sit down and eat. You could try eating your meals — breakfast and lunch — with your toddler as an example for her.

Toddlers also become quite erratic in their appetite, so you may find that one day she will eat everything in sight and then for the next three days she will eat barely anything. This is very normal behaviour. Because toddlers are on the go all the time, and growing and learning so many new things, the desire to eat will come and go. She will get enough food and you should offer every meal as you normally would and ensure that some of each meal is eaten.

## What types of food?

By this age your toddler should be eating most of the same foods you eat, minus the chilli and strong spices, and the texture should be lumpy, so cut up her food rather than mash or purée it. It is important to offer a baby different textures so they get used to eating regular food — that is, less puréed and more like older children eat. You should also be offering lots of different flavours as well as textures, so she starts to like different types of food and expands her palate. Remember, when introducing a new food that your baby might look like she does not like, often this is just a normal reaction to a new food. Keep presenting the new food regularly and she will get used to the new taste.

At this age most babies want to be involved in the feeding process so offer her finger food as well as the food that is being fed to her at that meal. The food should be more chunky, as I mentioned, and she might want to try to use a spoon and feed herself. Give her a spoon so she can try it.

She should now be getting protein twice a day and a couple of servings of fruit and vegetables as well. She is old enough to have wheat and cereal for breakfast and sandwiches for lunch can be a good alternative to what she might have been having previously. Other foods you can now offer include:

+ honey
+ strawberries
+ egg whites
+ cow's milk if you haven't already.

You should still avoid things that have a high risk of allergy or choking potential, such as:

✦ all types of nuts

✦ seeds and pips

✦ salt and sugar (purely because your child doesn't need these flavours)

✦ popcorn

✦ corn kernels.

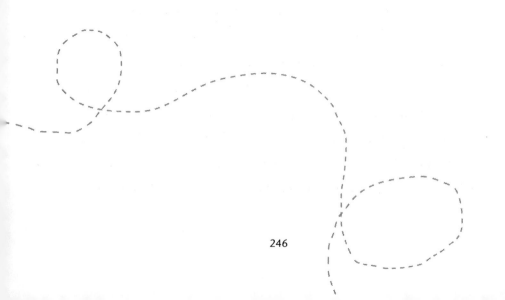

# Development and stimulation

It is during this time that things become interesting in other development areas as well. A toddler's development is rapid and as parents you will find that you have a whole new set of issues to deal with.

By this age your toddler will be very aware that she is a separate little person and acknowledge this by constantly saying the word 'me' or wanting things for herself. The notion of sharing is not possible as the world revolves around her, and she will like to let everyone know that. She may also start to use the word 'no' fairly frequently. So this is an important time to begin to set boundaries and teach her what is acceptable behaviour and what is not.

Someone once said to me that they were told that when a toddler was displaying unacceptable behaviour — in this case, biting his mother — that she was just to ignore it and continue on like nothing was happening. I completely disagree with this. A young child needs to be taught, by her parents, the difference between right and wrong, or how else will she learn? When she is doing something that is not acceptable, like biting, you need to tell her, in a firm voice, that that behaviour is not tolerated. And your reaction needs to be repeated every time she does something outside of what you deem acceptable. This is the way she will learn the rules and boundaries of her particular family.

When a family has boundaries that are reinforced, the child then learns these boundaries and becomes aware of what is expected of them. They are also aware of the consequences if they cross these boundaries.

If your child is putting her hand in the DVD player or about to crawl into the fire, you need to reinforce the boundary by saying 'no' and also moving her away from the thing you don't want her near. And you might have to do this 178 times every day but it is really important to reinforce your boundary because that is the way she will learn. You may also find yourself rearranging the house so that precious and dangerous items are out of her reach.

A young toddler can also start to display signs of frustration over what she wants to do and what she can actually do. This is often the first sign of a tantrum, although she will work up to being a great tantrum-thrower around two years of age. It is a good idea to sit down with your toddler and play with her, and show her how to do certain tasks over and over again. Toddlers love repetitive games, especially with an adult. She will not be interested in playing with other children and will often play on her own even when there are other children around.

Around 15 months a young child should start to walk, but this can happen as early as nine months and as late as 19 months. Her language skills will be increasing rapidly and she will start to repeat what you say to her and remember learnt words. When she sees an object like a dog — she will point at it and say what it is, but she may also get frustrated if you are not able to understand what she is trying to tell you.

## Developmental milestones

By 18 months your baby should:
+ want to explore her environment and touch and pull at everything she can get her hands on
+ express different emotions easily and swap quickly from one to another
+ show an aversion to strangers but be very attached to her main carers
+ have some distress when her parent/s leave her
+ start to walk
+ climb up onto low furniture or stairs
+ push something on wheels
+ be able to hold a pencil and scribble on paper
+ pick up objects
+ put one object on top of another
+ 'post' an object through an opening
+ babble loudly as if having a conversation
+ listen to what is being said to her and understand words like 'no' and 'stop'
+ point out objects when asked — for example, 'Where is the ball?'
+ know and use about six or more words.

## Playing with your baby

At this age some things you can do to entertain and stimulate your baby are:

+ sit with her and do puzzles
+ play with things she can push and pull, like knobs and buttons, trains and toys on a lead
+ read to her and teach her what the book is about — for example, 'This is a dog, what does a dog say?'
+ play with toys that imitate real objects like telephones, baby dolls, imitation food and cooking utensils
+ teach her to play on her own, so ensure every day that she has some playtime on her own.

## Safety issues

Because your child is now mobile and wanting to explore his environment you need to make sure that it is safe for him. One of the things around your home that can be a problem is stairs. Stairs should have a gate either at the top or the bottom, or both. If you live in a house with stairs then you need to teach your baby how to climb up and down safely. Babies of this age can learn, so you need to demonstrate how he should climb down backwards and climb up. Repeating this over and over will help him get it, but I would also continue to use gates until he is older and really able to manage stairs safely.

Other safety issues for babies of this age (and for most of their childhood) include:

- ✦ choking
- ✦ equipment like walkers
- ✦ falling off things
- ✦ drowning
- ✦ burns, including sunburn
- ✦ suffocation or strangulation.

So when your baby is moving around your house, you need to make sure there is nothing he can pull over on to himself, especially heavy items like televisions and chairs. Also put a safety cover on low power sockets that he might be able to stick something into.

Keep a keen eye out for small items around the house that your baby could put in his mouth and this includes toys with small parts. If you have older children with toys that have small parts then put them in a place where your baby cannot get at them.

Make sure all hot drinks and food are kept well out of your baby's reach as otherwise he could pull them on to himself. When bathing *never* leave your baby and always test the water temperature before putting him into the bath or shower.

You also need to keep all dangerous items like medicines and cleaning products out of reach of your baby. You can fit safety latches on kitchen and bathroom cupboards or keep them all up high where your baby can't get at them. Any kinds of cords, curtain ties, electrical leads or anything else that could cause strangulation need to be removed and kept way out of reach.

You should also have a look around the garden and outdoor areas to make sure there is nothing that your baby could hurt himself on. Babies and children should always wear sunscreen and a hat when going outdoors. It is a good idea to have a list of emergency numbers, such as the local children's hospital, the poisons information number and triple 0 close by and somewhere very visible, and to keep your first aid skills up to date.

Babies of this age should still be in a child restraint when travelling in the car and they should still be strapped in when in the pram.

## Setting boundaries and dealing with tantrums

Once your baby is around 12 months of age he might start to have what can only be described as tantrums. There is the common expression 'the terrible twos', but tantrums can actually start quite a bit earlier than this. I find girls can start having tantrums around ten months with boys starting a little later. It is difficult to rationalise with a young child but there are some things you can do to try to minimise the tantrums.

This is when you can start to teach your child about boundaries. When setting boundaries it is important to make sure it is something you can maintain, such as 'Don't pull the books off the shelf', or 'Don't hit'. Just like having rituals during the day with your routine, you can have rituals around boundaries. If your child is doing something he shouldn't then you need to tell him not to do it, and move him away. If he continues to do it then you need to continue to move him away from whatever he is doing while repeating the same word or phrase like 'No' or 'Hot'. If this 'ritual' happens every time he goes to do that thing he will learn that he is not to do it.

It is important to be consistent when you are setting and maintaining boundaries with your child. If you are wishy-washy with your rules or boundaries he will not know what he is supposed to do or not do. Your child will test or push a boundary and if he is able to get away with something because you are not firm with the boundary, then he will usually throw a tantrum until you give in, or else he will continue to do the wrong thing.

When a child throws a tantrum it is important to not give him the thing he is throwing the tantrum about. For example, if he is throwing a tantrum because you took something away from him that he should not be playing with or touching, then you should not give that thing back to him. You also should not offer 'bribes' to stop your child yelling or crying, like 'If you stop crying you can have a lolly'. This only teaches a child that if he behaves badly he will get a reward.

Children crave attention as they believe that the world revolves around them. This is not a bad thing but rather a normal part of development. But if your child can't get any good attention from you and throwing a tantrum gets your attention then he will learn pretty quickly that behaving like that works as well or better than not.

As mentioned above, you shouldn't reward bad behaviour, and it is absolutely true. If your child is behaving badly then you need to tell him what he is doing that you don't like, or if he is young then remove him from whatever he is doing. If your child is screaming and throwing himself on the floor then I recommend that you turn your back to him (after making sure he is not going to hurt himself), or sit away from him but within sight, and do not say anything. Once he has calmed down you can go to him and give him a hug and explain what he was doing that was not acceptable. Even when a child is very young I think it is respectful to tell him what he did that was crossing a boundary.

If you are out and it is not feasible to walk away from your child, then you should just ignore him as much as you can and put up with the screaming. Some people might stare but other parents will feel for you as most of them will have been in that situation at one time or another. Again, don't offer your child a reward to stop the tantrum, just keep doing what you were doing, as much as you can until he either calms down or you can get him home.

I am not a supporter of smacking children as I think it gives them the wrong message. You wouldn't hit the family dog or cat, so why would you hit your precious child? I also find that as children grow smacking is an ineffective means of discipline and usually only a compulsive reaction from the parent or carer. Plus, after you have smacked your child you feel awful about it. Remember, you are your child's role model and you would hate to see your child hit another child because that is the way he is disciplined at home.

Under the age of two children usually aren't sure what they have done wrong when they do it, so smacking them is really an unfair thing to do. Removing your child from what he is doing, and saying a firm 'No' or 'Stop' can be effective. You may have to repeat yourself over and over but he will catch on that it is something he is not supposed to be doing.

When disciplining your child, always keep your head about you and take a deep breath before you do anything. Try to imagine what your child would see and hear when you are maintaining the boundary and remember that he needs to learn what he is doing wrong and what the consequence is before he will stop doing it. And this will take time and repetition.

# Chapter 11

# Where to from here?

Hopefully you have found this book helpful and you have a baby who is a great sleeper and you as parents are confident and instinctive.

I have tried to make the book as practical as possible by including my philosophy on all aspects of the first 18 months of your child's life. The main thing I would reiterate is that above all else you should really try to enjoy these early days as much as you can. I know that sounds easy for me to say, but whatever is happening, whether it be sleep deprivation or a baby who won't eat her solids as much as you would like, there are things you can do to make it better. Many parents tell me that with their first baby they put up with no sleep for much longer than they needed to and now they are on their second baby there is no way they are going to do that again! But you actually don't have to put up with it at all.

You also need to remember that this time of your baby's life is really such a minuscule part of their life as a child, and so although when you are in the middle of it you feel like it will never end, when they are two or three or five you won't really remember the details at all. So I encourage you to not get too hung up on the little things.

It is important to watch and get to know your baby. Your baby is a unique individual, with her own little ways, so try not to compare her to other babies. Let her find her way in the world in her own way and her own time.

I have discussed instinctive parenting and if you can tap into your instincts about your baby then you will find parenting really rewarding. The little hiccups you may encounter along the way can be solved by relying on the instincts you have about your children. If you use them, along with a few tips from *Babybliss*, your experience and your baby's transition into the world will be a wonderful experience and one that you will cherish.

Don't wish this time to be over as it is so short: embrace it and go with it. At the end of it you will be a fabulous, instinctive parent who can help your friends and family and eventually your own children navigate their way through the whole experience with confidence.

As your children grow, always return to the things that are important — routine, ritual and instinct. Treat your children with respect always and watch and learn from them. Children are the most beautiful creatures; they are innocent and completely honest and have a most sincere joy for life. That is why I love my job so much!

# List of resources

# Feeding

If you are having issues with breastfeeding I would recommend you contact the Australian Breastfeeding Association, which has branches in every state. It is much better to seek help with feeding sooner rather than later.

Australian Breastfeeding Association (ABA)
www.breastfeeding.asn.au

Helpline numbers:

| | |
|---|---|
| ACT/Southern New South Wales | (02) 6258 8928 |
| New South Wales | (02) 8853 4999 |
| Queensland | (07) 3844 8977 or |
| | (07) 3844 8166 |
| Townsville | (07) 4723 5566 |
| Cairns | (07) 4058 0007 |
| Toowoomba | (07) 4639 2401 |
| South Australia and | (08) 8411 0050 |
| Northern Territory | |
| Northern Territory counsellor | (08) 8411 0301 |
| Tasmania | (03) 6223 2609 |
| Tasmania (North) | (03) 6331 2799 |
| Victoria | (03) 9885 0653 |
| Western Australia | (08) 9340 1200 |

Australian Lactation Consultants Association (ALCA)

www.alca.asn.au

Phone: (02) 6295 0384

Reflux Infants Support Association (RISA)

www.reflux.org.au

Phone: (07) 3229 1090 (Queensland)

## Government support agencies

Government support agencies can assist with any social, financial or health issues you may be experiencing.

Centrelink

www.centrelink.gov.au

Phone numbers:  1800 050 004

13 12 02 (multilingual enquiries)

1800 810 586 (TTY — teletypewriter for the hearing impaired)

Medicare

www.medicareaustralia.gov.au

Phone numbers: 13 20 11

13 14 50 (multilingual enquiries)

Federal Department of Families, Housing, Community Services
and Indigenous Affairs
www.facs.gov.au
Phone: 1800 670 305

Family Assistance Office
www.familyassist.gov.au
Phone numbers: 13 61 50
13 12 02 (multilingual enquiries)
1800 810 587 (TTY — teletypewriter for the
hearing impaired)

# Twins and multiple births

The more help the better if you are the parents of twins or
multiples. The Australian Multiple Birth Association has groups
in every state and the website is a great resource for information
from people who have experienced the joy and trials of having
more than one baby at the same time.

Australian Multiple Birth Association
www.amba.org.au
Phone: 1300 886 499

# Premature babies

Having a premature baby can result in a very stressful time for parents and families. Getting support from others who have experienced what you are going through is really important and very helpful.

L'il Aussie Prems
www.lilaussieprems.com.au
Phone: 0412 248 583

Austprem
www.austprem.org.au
Phone: 1300 BORN EARLY — 1300 267 632

National Premmie Foundation
www.prembaby.org.au
Phone: 1300 PREM BABY — 1300 773 622

## Parent support services

Good Beginnings is a national charity that works in partnership with communities to provide early childhood intervention services. It promotes children's resilience and engages in advocacy that builds the capacity of parents and carers.

Good Beginnings has a range of socially inclusive early childhood development services to help children and their families to flourish and in turn contribute to effective communities.

Good Beginnings
www.goodbeginnings.net.au
Phone: (02) 9211 6767

## Postnatal depression

Postnatal depression (PND) is very real and very debilitating. It is important to get as much help as you can if you are experiencing symptoms of PND. Beyond Blue is a national organisation to assist and support people and their families suffering from depression.

Beyond Blue
www.beyondblue.org.au
Phone: 1300 224 636

# Accidents and accident prevention

It is important to seek medical attention as soon as possible if your child is injured or sick. Have these numbers placed somewhere close to the home telephone and always make any carers aware of their existence.

Adverse Medicine Event Line
www.mater.org.au
Phone: 1300 134 237

Kidsafe Australia
www.kidsafe.com.au

Poisons Information Centre
Phone: 13 11 26

# Babybliss
# Newborn
# Log

## Babybliss Newborn Log

| Time feed started | How long on left breast? | How long on right breast? | Bowels (tick) | Wet nappy (tick) | Awake from when to when? | Total awake time | Slept for how long? (From when to when?) | Total time asleep |
|---|---|---|---|---|---|---|---|---|
| | | | | | | | | |
| | | | | | | | | |
| | | | | | | | | |
| | | | | | | | | |
| | | | | | | | | |
| | | | | | | | | |
| | | | | | | | | |
| | | | | | | | | |
| | | | | | | | | |
| | | | | | | | | |
| | | | | | | | | |
| | | | | | | | | |

## Babybliss Newborn Log

| Time feed started | How long on left breast? | How long on right breast? | Bowels (tick) | Wet nappy (tick) | Awake from when to when? | Total awake time | Slept for how long? (From when to when?) | Total time asleep |
|---|---|---|---|---|---|---|---|---|
| | | | | | | | | |
| | | | | | | | | |
| | | | | | | | | |
| | | | | | | | | |
| | | | | | | | | |
| | | | | | | | | |
| | | | | | | | | |
| | | | | | | | | |
| | | | | | | | | |
| | | | | | | | | |
| | | | | | | | | |
| | | | | | | | | |
| | | | | | | | | |

## Babybliss Newborn Log

| Time feed started | How long on left breast? | How long on right breast? | Bowels (tick) | Wet nappy (tick) | Awake from when to when? | Total awake time | Slept for how long? (From when to when?) | Total time asleep |
|---|---|---|---|---|---|---|---|---|
| | | | | | | | | |
| | | | | | | | | |
| | | | | | | | | |
| | | | | | | | | |
| | | | | | | | | |
| | | | | | | | | |
| | | | | | | | | |
| | | | | | | | | |
| | | | | | | | | |
| | | | | | | | | |
| | | | | | | | | |
| | | | | | | | | |
| | | | | | | | | |

## Babybliss Newborn Log

| Time feed started | How long on left breast? | How long on right breast? | Bowels (tick) | Wet nappy (tick) | Awake from when to when? | Total awake time | Slept for how long? (From when to when?) | Total time asleep |
|---|---|---|---|---|---|---|---|---|
| | | | | | | | | |
| | | | | | | | | |
| | | | | | | | | |
| | | | | | | | | |
| | | | | | | | | |
| | | | | | | | | |
| | | | | | | | | |
| | | | | | | | | |
| | | | | | | | | |
| | | | | | | | | |
| | | | | | | | | |
| | | | | | | | | |

## Babybliss Newborn Log

| Time feed started | How long on left breast? | How long on right breast? | Bowels (tick) | Wet nappy (tick) | Awake from when to when? | Total awake time | Slept for how long? (From when to when?) | Total time asleep |
|---|---|---|---|---|---|---|---|---|
| | | | | | | | | |
| | | | | | | | | |
| | | | | | | | | |
| | | | | | | | | |
| | | | | | | | | |
| | | | | | | | | |
| | | | | | | | | |
| | | | | | | | | |
| | | | | | | | | |
| | | | | | | | | |
| | | | | | | | | |
| | | | | | | | | |
| | | | | | | | | |

## Babybliss Newborn Log

| Time feed started | How long on left breast? | How long on right breast? | Bowels (tick) | Wet nappy (tick) | Awake from when to when? | Total awake time | Slept for how long? (From when to when?) | Total time asleep |
|---|---|---|---|---|---|---|---|---|
| | | | | | | | | |
| | | | | | | | | |
| | | | | | | | | |
| | | | | | | | | |
| | | | | | | | | |
| | | | | | | | | |
| | | | | | | | | |
| | | | | | | | | |
| | | | | | | | | |
| | | | | | | | | |
| | | | | | | | | |
| | | | | | | | | |

# THANK YOU

There are many, many people who have helped me enormously during the writing of this book. First and foremost are all the babies and their wonderful families who I see and talk to every day. Over the time of writing this book and the whole time Babybliss has been around, I have learnt so much more than I ever knew before about babies, and it is all from seeing and experiencing different families and their particular situations. So a huge thank you for letting me into your homes and your lives. I need to thank one family in particular who set the wheels in motion for me to write this book. Andrew, Karen, Lucas and Nathaniel, thank you. To Ginny and Nikki a big thanks for getting on board with Babybliss and helping us get the word out there. Thank you, thank you, thank you to Jo and Mel from HarperCollins for all your advice and support to a *very* novice author who thought she really couldn't write (and was probably right). And to Ben for helping me get started. To my friends who I love more than anything, particularly Sara, Margot, Sally, Phil, Maria and Davey (and their families) who are my biggest cheerleaders — and also fabulous parents (or parents-to-be). And finally my family, who are a neverending source of support and love. Mum and Michael, Lisa, Em, Jono and their wonderful families, I sincerely thank you for your advice, your constructive eye and most importantly the love you show me every day.

# BABYBLISS TESTIMONIALS

Our family can never repay Jo for what she has done for us. Jo has changed our lives and we are so grateful to her. I really feel the need to try and get across to families that what Jo does is an investment and whatever the costs involved far outweigh the end result which is your lives are changed forever. When you see what Jo does, you'll ask yourself why you didn't get her help earlier. Jo knows what's she's talking about and the proof is out there. Three things that really stand out in my mind about Jo and why I'd highly recommend her to anyone are that she is able to teach your baby to self settle without using controlled crying, that what she taught me with my first born child meant I knew what to do when our second baby came along and this made the most amazing difference the second time around, and finally, no matter how busy Jo was, she always found the time to email or phone me and answer any questions I had. This showed me that she really does care about the families she works with. Jo has been working with families for years. I cannot imagine there is a baby out there that Jo couldn't help. She's the only person I know of who can really help you with your baby. I honestly can't speak highly enough of her.

**Sam**

Our nine-month-old son Sean had developed a bad habit of waking up three to four times a night and I would always use the dummy or a bottle to re-settle. Because of these extra bottles at night, Sean would refuse all milk during the day and then started to refuse his daytime sleeps too. Needless to say, our lives were out of control and so, sleep deprived and stressed out, we contacted Jo. Sean warmed to Jo straight away and I immediately felt a sense of relief that first night as I knew that our lives were about to change for the better. Jo stayed with us for three nights and Sean now sleeps 12 hours each night and three hours each day. I no longer dread bedtime as he settles himself to sleep within five minutes every time — what a transformation! For me, the best part about Jo's work is that she gave me the skills and the confidence to deal with Sean's night waking and to also understand his sleeping patterns. Even if Sean does wake up during the night, I now know what to do and I know that it works so I can let go of all the anxiety that I previously felt. Thank you, Jo, for helping us and our baby learn these skills. Our lives have improved immeasurably and we are so grateful.

**Nathan and Nicole**

My wife and I had difficulty with Ollie's sleep, who, after three months, decided to add multiple wakes during the night. By six months of age he was still waking multiple times during the night even after we cut several of the feeds out. Although we would both wake, a good portion of the settling for those night wakes fell into my domain. Working long hours and faced with a restless baby during the night was wearing me out. But who am I to complain? At least I got to go to work! Essentially we were both sleep deprived and getting on each other's nerves. Ollie was very dummy dependent and essentially woke every time he lost it during the night. We tried tying spare dummies to the end of his muslins and encouraged him to find them during the night. No luck. We tried cutting the night feeds out. No luck. My wife found Jo but as a natural skeptic I had my doubts as to the level of success she would have. But I was very quickly proved wrong. Jo was gentle yet assertive with our Ollie. In fact, he became very fond of her. After the end of night three (Jo's last night) we were fearful of the status quo returning. But it didn't. On our first night without Jo, he woke a couple of times but self settled. Since then we have enjoyed a full night of sleep every night. He goes to bed at 7 pm and does not wake until 6 am. I am now ready for number two!

**KW**

Hi Jo!

Just thought about you this morning and wanted to send you a quick message to thank you sooooo much for your services in November for our youngest cherub, Grace. She is still sleeping peacefully through the night and our lives have returned to normal so much so that we are now trying for another little one (something we would NEVER have thought about six months ago when you visited). Her routine is fabulous, she is lots and lots of fun and the happiest little girl around. She turns one on Friday and this has been the most amazing six months of our lives since you helped us through her sleep (or lack of sleep) problems.

Thanks again, you are an absolute star and we talk about your services to anyone who will listen (I am on my soapbox on a regular basis). It still brings a tear to the eye to think about how much you changed our lives and educated us on what she needed. Olivia still mentions the 'baby whisperer' who came and helped get Gracie to sleep.

**Michelle**

After getting advice left, right and centre about how to get Daniel to have better sleeping habits, nothing was working. We tried the community clinics but found that after Daniel was six months we had nowhere to turn to. We called Jo and she came to stay with us for three days and two nights. Daniel learnt to settle himself to sleep in the first day AND he slept right through the night as well! Jo helped us get Daniel into a healthy eating and sleeping routine which made the whole challenge of parenthood so much easier and allowed us to enjoy Daniel more as we weren't so stressed and sleep deprived. Jo left us with so much confidence that having been a sufferer of PND I was advised I could come off my medication a few weeks after Jo had left. All of my friends who were great at giving us advice to us at the beginning are now asking us for advice and I direct them to Jo and her website! The best reason I can give to use Jo is that she is willing to work with you and your values using a method that you are comfortable with in your own home where you and your baby are comfortable.

**Suzi**

As the mother of one-year-old twin boys, it was not uncommon for me to dread sundown and wake in the morning after three to four hours of sleep not knowing how I was going to make it through the day! We all think that sleep deprivation is the downside to motherhood; however, after too many bad days with children who I knew needed more sleep, my husband and I called on Jo for advice. What a difference she has made to our lives! As Jo has explained, sleeping well really is a skill that can be learnt. Before Jo arrived, the boys bedtime was at 8.30 pm with several awake periods throughout the night before needing to be rocked back to sleep. We were simply going through the motions to get to 6am. Now, the boys are sleeping from 7 pm until 7 am with a great sleep in the day, all thanks to Jo. We found Jo to be the most caring and loving stranger that our children would ever meet. She is compassionate and has such a calm confidence that as soon as you meet her you know that sleeping is going to improve. All of our friends and family cannot believe what a difference the new sleep routines have made to our lives and I cannot speak highly enough of her services. We feel that Jo is still committed to us and, although it has been only a few days since Jo was with us, she has already checked in to make sure that our twins are keeping up with their newfound sleep. Thank you again, Jo, for having the patience to come to our home and save us from the sleeplessness! You have enabled us to appreciate our beautiful boys again and for this we will always be indebted.

**Amie**

# Notes

# Notes

# Notes

To find out more about
Jo Ryan's Babybliss services, visit
www.babybliss.com.au